THE MODERN FLOWER PRESS

Library of Congress Control Number: 2022932221

ISBN: 978-1-4197-6467-7
eISBN: 978-1-64700-830-7

Design by Zoë Bather

First published in Great Britain in 2022 by William Collins, an imprint of HarperCollinsPublishers

Published in the United States in 2022 by Abrams, an imprint of ABRAMS.

Printed and bound in Bosnia-Herzegovina by GPS Group
10 9 8 7 6 5 4 3 2 1

ABRAMS The Art of Books
195 Broadway, New York, NY 10007
abramsbooks.com

MIX
Paper from responsible sources
FSC™ C007454

Melissa Richardson & Amy Fielding

THE MODERN FLOWER PRESS

Capturing the Beauty of Nature

Abrams, New York

A thing of beauty is a joy for ever:
Its loveliness increases; it will never
Pass into nothingness.
"Endymion," John Keats (1795–1821)

Long ago I opened a secondhand book and a pressed flower fluttered out and lay in the sunshine leaking through the blinds that spring morning. It was as delicate as a butterfly's wing; its colours barely faded; the petals papery and translucent. I wondered who had pressed that flower? Were they trying to capture a precious moment long forgotten? Only the flower remained. Whatever it had meant to the presser was lost, but the pansy, released from the pages of the book after so many years, was as beautiful as the day it was picked.

A pressed flower is like a memory; and like memories they change and fade over time. Flowers, with their brief little performance in the sun, have reminded many of the great poets and thinkers of their own mortality. Their fragility is a sharp and barely acknowledged pain. As the flower opens, it has already begun its dance with death. By cutting a flower and pressing it we are extending its life and defying nature. We have in some way helped them to escape their inevitable fate.

Melissa Richardson and Amy Fielding are joint directors of renowned London florist JamJar Flowers and its sister company, JamJar Edit.

Amy and I came together by chance when she knocked on the door of the JamJar studio around five years after I started the business. As it happens we are pretty much opposites, as much as I am mercurial and messy and careering towards seventy, Amy is just embarking on married life with her first baby, fantastically organized and meticulous about detail. Our strengths and weaknesses balance us out. Our combined love of the natural world has kept us on track and we have built a business together in JamJar Edit—our online shop and flower-pressing studio. We kind of stumbled into the world of pressed flowers, but we quickly fell in love with the process, and now we want to share some of our adventures with you here.

So we invite you to come with us on a journey of discovery and preservation. As well as being something of a manual for those who want to try their hand at flower pressing, we have tried to cover all aspects of the craft that are interesting to us. We have considered the people who pressed flowers for practical reasons—to record a plant or document a journey of discovery; those who press for sentimental reasons, to try to preserve a precious moment; or those who do so as part of an artistic practice. We have explored all the ways in which we could lift this craft out of its traditional confines and make it more relevant and modern, taking the most simple craft and elevating it to a higher level. This is where we believe it deserves to be; not tucked away in dusty Victorian herbaria, but adorning the walls of modern British homes and recalling us to nature with stunning visual artworks.

The idea for this book took shape during the Covid-19 lockdown, when so much of our lives, including our business, seemed to be disappearing before our eyes. In March 2019, as we strived to make sense out of the crazy situation, we started to sketch out a proposal for a book. We felt we had a story that people might like to hear and we had all the time in the world to think about how we could tell it. So although this book was born out of panic and fear, it also grew from a longing to rediscover the beauty in the world around us. As lockdown continued, we found that nature was pretty much what we were left with and that wasn't too awful a proposition after all. Research for this book has led us down some fantastic rabbit holes, from which we emerged blinking into the sunlight and yearning to know more.

We hope you will enjoy all the ideas and projects in these pages and that it may encourage some of you to try pressing flowers for yourselves. It is a most rewarding pastime and one that we are so pleased to have pursued and brought into the modern world of flower artistry.

READER'S DIGEST ENCYCLOPAEDIA OF GARDEN PLANTS AND FLOWERS
PANTONE
100 Postcards

the ULTIMATE FLORAL COLLECTION
BLOOMS
A-Z GARDEN PLANTS A-J DK
A-Z GARDEN PLANTS K-Z DK
ENCYCLOPEDIA OF GARDEN PLANTS AND FLOWERS

Story

NIGELLA

Light love-in-a-mist, by the midsummer moon misguided,
Scarce seen in the twilight garden if gloom insist,
Seems vainly to seek for a star whose gleam has derided
Light love-in-a-mist.
"Love in a Mist," Algernon Swinburne (1837–1909)

There is nothing more pleasing for growing and pressing than *Nigella damascena*. All you need is a patch of sparse gravel and a plump seedhead begged from a friend, then you can simply scatter the angular black seeds about. They will come up in May, blue as the summer sky, the beautiful flowers nestled among the feathery leaves, ethereal and pretty—flower faeries dancing in the breeze.

When it comes to pressing, nigella is a JamJar favourite, almost invariably successful and a very good flower to start your experiments with. Nigella is part of the Ranunculaceae family, which makes it first cousin to the buttercup. It is native to southern Europe, North Africa, and Southwest Asia and likes damp, neglected land, which is probably why it loves our London gravel garden so much. En masse, the feathery leaves look like a green mist, with the starry flowers dotted through like hundreds of fluttering, tiny blue butterflies. This delicate foliage fanning out around each flower is how it gets its charming familiar name, "love-in-a-mist."

There are many different varieties, and although most are blue, you can also get nigella in pink and white. "Persian Jewels" is a good cultivar to grow because it has all three colours in one seed pack. First cousin to *Nigella damascena* is *Nigella sativa*, also known as black cumin or kalonji/kalanji. (The word "nigella" stems from the Latin "*niger*," meaning black.) The black seeds are used in cookery in Pakistan, India, and across the Middle East. The fragrant seeds have notes of onion, black pepper, and oregano, and in Palestine they are used to make *qizha* paste, which has a sharp, bitter taste with an underlying sweetness. It is an ingredient in tahini and various breads and pastries.

There is evidence that *Nigella sativa* seeds have been highly prized for thousands of years. They were found in Egyptian tombs and discovered in a Hittite flask in Turkey that is more than 4,000 years old. Rather surprisingly, despite their history, there are no myths or legends that I can find surrounding the flower. Its medical uses also seem to be minimal—although we know that nigella seeds were used in ancient times as a medicine for shortness of breath and low blood pressure.

After the flower is over, a wonderfully sculptural seedhead swells. It is bulbous, sometimes striped with red or purple, with a perky, spiky crown. I think this is where the plant gets its less-popular familiar name of "devil-in-a-bush," or "chase-the-devil."

At JamJar we love using the seedheads as well as the flowers in arrangements, and after they have been dried (simply by being hung upside down in a warm dry place) we use the pods in everlasting dried-flower pieces, where they add form and texture. They are as easy to dry as they are to grow, but always remember to leave a few in the garden to self-seed, so you can be certain of next year's crop.

Nigella has so much to commend it; it is simple to grow, to dry, and to press, and all these attributes make it a beautiful and necessary flower in the JamJar pantheon.

Project

MULBERRY

In August 2014—just a few weeks before the Spring/Summer collections were due to be shown at London Fashion Week—we received a call from the prestigious British fashion label, Mulberry, to discuss an idea for their show invitations. We knew this would be an interesting commission—the previous year Mulberry had collaborated with iconic English brand Wedgwood, who made bespoke teacup and saucer sets to send out to guests ahead of the show, each complementing the colours of the Spring collection.

We were invited to Mulberry to discuss the project and preview their printed fabrics. The company wanted to incorporate pressed flowers into the design for their show invitations, inspired by the floral prints in their collection. Swathes of fabric in cornflower blues, navy, and white were printed with graphic illustrations of Queen Anne's Lace *(Ammi majus)*, nigella, delphiniums, and cornflowers. The idea was to send out vintage copies of *The Observer's Book of Wild Flowers* to each of their guests, with pressed flowers resembling those used in the collection slipped into the cover as if they'd been pressed inside the pages of the book and long forgotten.

Flower pressing wasn't something we had been asked to do before, but we thought, how hard could it be? Hadn't everyone pressed flowers with their granny when they were little?

Our research suggested that the flower-pressing process would take four to six weeks, but of course, this being fashion, we were given about half that time to complete the job. Each invitation was to include around seven pressed flowers, and there were 700 invitations to be sent—so that meant we needed to press just under 5,000 flower heads in total, with a bit of contingency. The pressure was on.

The specification of *Ammi majus* was important as it featured repeatedly throughout Mulberry's collection. When pressed, its dainty white flowers look like elegant lacework. Blue bee delphiniums, cornflowers, antique blue hydrangeas, and nigella reflected the prints and colours and provided a pretty range of textures and tones. Being late summer, these were all available in abundance from the flower market. They also had quite flat heads, which was to our advantage as this meant they would press quicker than other, more complex, flower varieties.

We had one tiny flower press in the studio, an old one Melissa had had for years, which we filled quickly with our first experiments. We soon learned that careful placement of the flowers inside the press was important to achieve good results. Taking time to flatten out any creases in the petals or to remove untidy leaves saved time later. The hydrangea florets pressed very quickly and kept their colour—as did the electric-blue delphinium heads.

THE OBSERVER'S BOOK
OF
GARDEN
MULBERRY
INVITES YOU TO VIEW
THE
SPRING SUMMER 2015
CATWALK COLLECTION

We were especially pleased with the nigella, which came out of the press with perfectly preserved flower heads and pretty frilly collars. Still, we only had two or three weeks to produce thousands of pressed flowers. With time absolutely not on our side, we tried all sorts of methods to speed up the process—ironing flowers between layers of greaseproof paper, laying them on hot tiles in the oven. We had even read about a microwave flower press, but we thought that was a step too far…

One of our studio neighbours had a heavy iron book press, which we commandeered to fill with layers of blotting paper and hundreds of flower heads. It was a bit brutal for flower pressing, but it was a handsome thing, which also worked perfectly for Mulberry's press shots and proved to be one of our favourite props. We ordered stacks more flower presses online, filled them, and took them home where we could keep a close eye on progress, hoping the warmth of our houses would speed up the drying process.

We didn't need to press long stems, as the *Observer* books are tiny, which meant we could fit a lot of heads into each press. Hydrangeas were separated into tiny florets, delphinium heads were snipped from the main stem to be pressed as individual flowers. In every press we had failures—some flowers came out mouldy, some petals had turned brown, some were just an ugly mess. But for all the failures, there were many more successes. It seemed

to be going well, our stock was building fairly rapidly, but then the guys at the flower market started sending buckets of *Ammi visnaga* instead of *Ammi majus*, as the latter was now apparently "over" for the season, just like that. *Ammi visnaga* has a much juicier, fatter umbel, which when flattened out becomes enormous. We tried flattening them anyway, only to find a horrible soggy mess when we opened the presses a few days later. Fortunately, *Ammi majus* suddenly appeared in the market again, like magic. It wasn't over after all, and we somehow managed to press enough heads to complete the job on time.

The invitations were printed on pale blue paper and wrapped around the cover of each book, tied in place with blue-and-white-striped baker's twine, then tucked into a neat kraft-paper postage box, complete with bespoke Mulberry stamps echoing the prints in the collection. Despite the frantic turnaround and our lack of knowledge, we had managed to pull off the job and the finished result looked absolutely gorgeous.

We are forever grateful to Mulberry for opening our eyes to this beautiful craft. Each time we opened a press in those early days of the job we learned a little bit more about the process, and in turn we fell completely in love with it. Little did we know that this would be the start of such a fascinating journey of botanical discovery for us.

Story

HELLEBORE

They arrive in the garden in early spring, with their lovely muted colours ranging from deep purple through plums, pinks, and greens, to white fading into pale pink. They suit the dim light in the garden. The hellebore's familiar name of Christmas Rose, or Lenten Rose, came about because of the time at which it appears in the garden and in the wild.

Despite the shape of the flower, they are not members of the rose family, but of the buttercup, or *Ranunculaceae*, family. There are over twenty species and many hybrids. They were first named by Carl Linnaeus (see page 32) in 1753. The name *Helleborus* means harmful food, translated from the Greek "*helein*," meaning to kill, and "*bora*," meaning food. Not all hellebores are poisonous, but it is probably the toxic ones that have given them their dark reputation.

Pedanius Dioscorides, a Greek physician living in the first century CE, wrote a five-volume botanical text, *De Materia Medica*, in which he described the medicinal qualities of over 600 plants. Dioscorides has hellebores down for treating insanity and melancholy, as well as for use as a purge. Grinding the roots into a powder and ingesting it induced vomiting but also, in larger doses, death.

Sometimes at JamJar, rather unkindly, we call them hellish bores. It is annoying to have to lie down in a damp and soggy border in February, or under a vase of flowers, to see the often exquisite, freckled, downturned faces of the temperamental hellebore. You can cut the flowers and float them in a bowl of water to admire the many varieties, and while this works well, it isn't madly to our taste. One of the prettiest gardens I know has hellebores planted on a slope so that you can actually see their lovely flowers as you walk the woodland path below. Today, clever horticulturists have developed hellebores that lift their heads up, but their natural inclination is to be downcast.

For florists, hellebores are not always easy to use; the downturned heads and tendency to wilt and sulk once cut makes them a risky choice. Not all flowers enjoy sharing a vase with hellebores, and if the hellebore does well the others often fail around it. More often the hellebore collapses limply within twenty-four hours of being cut. However, there are exceptions that last extremely well, such as "Magnificent Bells," a firm JamJar favourite, and "Ivory Prince," who holds his head up beautifully.

It is interesting to note that the colourful part of the flower that we would assume are its petals are in fact sepals—modified leaves that encase the developing flower bud. The actual petals are a tiny little frill around the stamens—the pollen part of the plant. Once the stamens and petals have fallen, the sepals become strong and waxy and the seedhead forms. These sepals do not lose much colour, which gives them a long season in the garden when little else is going on.

One of the more interesting stories about hellebores is also the first recorded instance of chemical warfare. In the sixth century CE, Delphi was the seat of Pythia—the Oracle who had to be consulted on all major decisions in the ancient world. To get to this sacred site by sea, pilgrims arrived at Kirrha, a thriving port on the Gulf of Corinth. The Kirrhaen citizens took advantage of the pilgrims by imposing exorbitant taxes on them, then robbing them and abusing their women on their return from the temple. Eventually, Delphi declared war on Kirrha and so began the First Sacred War. The citizens of Kirrha locked themselves behind their fortified walls and a siege began. According to Thessalus, the attackers eventually found a secret water pipe supplying the citadel after it was broken under a horse's hoof. The allies then poisoned the water with powdered hellebore, rendering the Kirrhaens helpless with diarrhoea and vomiting and enabling the allies to enter the city and massacre the entire population.

Another hellebore legend has it that Alexander the Great, who died aged thirty-two, was poisoned by the flower, either by his enemies, or because he was using it as a purge for an illness. And in Homer's *Odyssey*, the hero Odysseus used hellebore to poison the tips of his arrows.

Hellebores also feature in witchcraft, appearing alongside belladonna and mandrake as a powerful potion or poison in rites of exorcism and curses.

Magic potions made from the hellebore root aid a witch's ability to fly; the plants are also protected by birds and provide a portal to the Underworld. According to Pliny the Elder, a naturalist writing in the first century CE, the plant needed to be gathered with many elaborate ceremonies. First, a circle is traced around the hellebore with a sword, then the person who is harvesting it has to face east and offer up incantations to the gods asking for permission to uproot the plant. If an eagle flies overhead when the plant is being lifted, so legend goes, the harvester will die within the year. I am pleased to be able to confirm that I don't think this can be true. We have lifted many hellebores —roots and all—in the presence of many birds, without obvious ill-effects!

Hellebores grow in the shadows and thrive in the darkest months of the year, when the days are short and there is little else to see in the garden. Looking at the black hellebore, *Helleborus officinalis*, it is easy to understand how their gothic appearance and poisonous roots have inspired the many dark and sinister stories that surround them.

But the ominous and difficult reputation of hellebores is forgiven when it comes to pressing. They are the dream; they hold their shape and colour beautifully and, of course, we can easily manipulate those beautiful heads so that they stare us straight in the face, as they rarely do when they are growing in the ground.

Flower Press
Handmade in London

PRESSING TOOLS

To get started with flower pressing you just need a few basic items that are easy to get from stationery or craft shops.

FLOWER PRESS

We press most of our flowers in a standard-sized flower press—36 × 28cm (14 × 11 inches)—which fits pieces of blotting paper and card comfortably. For larger specimens we make our own flower presses using long MDF boards with holes drilled in the four corners and at intervals down the length for large screws. If you don't have a press, you can replicate this using several heavy books!

SCREWS, WING NUTS, WASHERS

Most flower presses come complete with fittings; the washers help protect the wooden top and bottom layers from damage when tightly screwing the wing nuts.

BLOTTING PAPER & CARD

When you buy a press it will come with paper and card, but it's helpful to have spares to replace damp sheets during pressing. Blotting paper is the best option, as it absorbs the moisture from the flowers, while card acts as a barrier to stop moisture seeping through the layers of paper. The thicker the paper, the better.

SCISSORS

A pair of sharp scissors is essential for snipping the ends of your stems. Japanese Niwaki scissors are great for precision.

MASKING TAPE

We use masking tape to label our presses once full. This allows us to change the labels easily when we empty a press.

PENCIL

Used for labelling. Write the flower types and date of pressing onto your masking tape to keep track of your pressings.

PAPER TOWELS

Use to dab moisture from flower stems before pressing.

Story

HERBARIUM

An herbarium is simply a collection of pressed and dried flowers, individually mounted and carefully labelled. Although not created specifically for artistic reasons, the flowers are often breathtakingly beautiful, even when viewed hundreds of years after the plants were gathered.

It was after a visit to a local small herbarium at the South London Botanical Institute that we decided to make our own collection of pressed flowers. Although our motive was to press specimens that we could make into artworks, rather than for scientific research, we were inspired and started to fill our archive boxes with flowers for as yet unplanned artwork.

The first herbaria were created long before photography existed, largely in order to record what plants looked like and to name them. Specimens were carefully selected to have a bud, a seedhead, a fully formed flower, and often roots, too. They were then labelled with the location where they were found, the nature of their habitat, when and by whom the plant was collected, and their colour was noted. Although artists were also frequently taken on plant-finding missions, their work could never be as perfectly botanically accurate and reliable as the pressed plant. This is also true of photography, which can be manipulated much more easily than a living flower simply pressed.

There is something magical about gazing at a plant that was pressed many centuries earlier. It is so easy to muse on its life when all the evidence is there for you to see. To imagine its first struggle through the surface of the soil, its growth into a mature plant somewhere far away, withstanding the vagaries of harsh weather and rain, and then to imagine again the arrival of the collector, cutting and pressing the flower and taking careful records. All these images flash into my mind's eye when looking at herbarium specimens.

There's nothing more charming than seeing a little wild strawberry, for example, with fruit, flower, and roots intact, suspended in time and strapped down with a little strip of tape, and reading the old-fashioned spidery writing next to it, telling you all about its known life. Even the imperfections, brown leaves, and insect damage only add to the story. Sometimes it seems the plant is calling out to you: "Look at me. My whole life is here if you will only look closely."

Carl Linnaeus said, "an herbarium is better than any illustration; every botanist should make one." He himself had a collection of around 14,000 specimens at the time of his death, which was then purchased by James Edward Smith, who founded the Linnaean Society in 1788. The Linnean Society was established "to inform, involve, and inspire people about nature and its significance," and the society is still very much operational to this day at its home in Burlington House, London.

Herbaria have many practical uses and are of fundamental importance to science. Here are some of the main reasons for the plant collections kept in herbaria around the world:

1. For species identification and taxonomy.
2. To establish the provenance of a plant.
3. To catalogue and identify flora and record the changes in vegetation over time.
4. For the study of geographic distributions and habitats of plants.
5. As a record of plants that have become extinct, which also acts as an aid for scientists to track climate change and the effects of human impact on native species.
6. To provide a source of plant DNA and an aid to botanists trying to determine and control invasive species.
7. As an aid to seed collection. Any seed entering the Millennium Seed Bank in Sussex, home to over 2.3 billion seeds from around the world, must have a pressed specimen to accompany it.

Primula
Rose Leaves
Scabious
Blue Scabious
Sea Lavender
Snake - Head Fritill
Stitchwort
Strawberry

The first record of an herbarium being created for scholarly purposes was made by Luca Ghini (1490–1556). Ghini was an Italian physician and botanist who was responsible for the first botanical garden in Europe. He called his pressed and dried plants his *hortus siccus*, or "dried garden." A scholar and a university lecturer, Ghini's idea for preserving the plants from his garden was really so that he could continue to lecture on botany and plant diversity with practical demonstrations through the winter months while most plants lay dormant. He discovered an innovative method for preserving plants by means of pressing them between sheets of absorbent paper, adding pressure to remove the moisture. Then, once dry, he mounted them with glue onto the blank pages of a book to form a practical research tool for his students. Sadly, none of Ghini's original herbarium survives today, but plants preserved by his pupils, such as Gherardo Cibo, are still in existence. Francesco Perolini, certainly a correspondent if not a pupil of Ghini, made one of the most charming herbaria still extant. Known simply as *En Tibi*, it is a large, beautiful book of pressings covering 473 species. The full title translated from the Latin is: "*Here, for you, a Smiling Garden of Everlasting Flowers*."

Ghini's contemporary, a German botanist, explorer, and plant collector called Leonhard Rauwolf, travelled to Western Asia and Turkey and created four volumes of pressed and preserved plants. Some of the pages had a thick border of coloured wallpaper to allow room for some of the more exotic and bulky pieces he had collected on his travels. These two herbaria were greatly prized and led quite a chequered life, being owned, at one point, by the Habsburg Emperor Rudolf II (1552–1612), from whose palace they were stolen and taken to Bavaria in 1620. They were stolen again by the Swedes, during the Thirty Years War (1618–48), and eventually ended up in the collection of the botanically minded Queen Christina of Sweden, who later gave the collection to her librarian, Isaac Vossius. Vossius donated both the *En Tibi* and the Rauwolf Collection to Leiden University, where they remain. This journey shows you not only how much these scholarly works were desired as botanical curiosities but, I suspect, also how much they were valued as items of great beauty.

After the deprivations of the Dark Ages, when learning was actively forbidden by the Catholic Church and empirical enquiry was closed down, came the burgeoning of intellectual and artistic expression that we call the Renaissance. The Renaissance was a period during the fifteenth and sixteenth centuries of great social change—it came as a shaft of light, a burst of new ideas and scientific discovery, bringing with it such innovations as the use of perspective in paintings, the creation of the telescope, the microscope and the herbarium.

There are some 800 herbariums in Europe, more than anywhere else in the world, which is largely down to the climate of this continent and the passion for travel in the eighteenth century. Climatically, for at least four months of the year most European plants are largely dormant, and in more moist and humid climates the specimens were more likely to rot. There is now a lot of controversy about the way plants were collected from foreign lands and brought back to Europe over centuries, often to benefit the patrons of the explorers. Native people of the countries from which plants were plundered were rarely, if ever, compensated, or even asked, before their precious resources were taken and used to enrich Western civilizations. Today this is known as biopiracy, and it is illegal. When a plant is said to have been "discovered" by a botanist, it will have obviously been well known to the natives of the country in which it was "found" for centuries. The directors of herbaria around the world are now doing their best to relabel and retell the stories of their plant collections.

Of course, the Europeans weren't the only ones curating information about plants and recording their medical uses, or creating naming systems—known as nomenclature. In China, India, and the Islamic world, texts with details of plants have been compiled for thousands of years, although more usually with text and illustrations than with pressed species. The pressing of flowers is perhaps less important in countries where the climate pro-

vides species more or less all year round. The Aztecs had massive plant-specimen libraries, all of which were destroyed by the European invasion under Hernán Cortés. Montezuma, the Aztec king, kept zoological and botanical gardens, which were vastly superior to those of his contemporaries in Europe. A huge source of knowledge was lost after the invasion, except for *Libellus de Medicinalibus Indorum Herbis*—a little book of Indian herbs written about thirty years after the Spanish Conquest by Martin de la Cruz and translated into Latin by Juan Badianus. It became known as the Bardianus Manuscript and was an important document, but the wonderful illustrations are highly stylized and therefore inaccurate, making them less useful than pressed species.

From the immaculate Mutis Collection housed in the Botanical Gardens in Madrid, to the National Herbarium in Paris, these herbaria tend to have fascinating histories. The latter houses the collection of Alexander von Humboldt and Aimé Bonpland, two European botanists who had sent precious specimens to friend and mentor Carl Willdenhow in Germany. After Willdenhow's death, his collection was sold to the herbarium of Berlin's Botanical Gardens, which, in 1940, was one of the largest and most important in the world. It contained some four million species collected over 175 years. During World War II, many specimens, including those collected by Humboldt and Willdenow, were moved to a mine shaft near Bleicherode, in Central Germany, for safekeeping. Fortunately, as it turned out, because on 1 March 1943 the herbarium received a direct hit from an Allied bomb and most of the collection was lost to fire and water damage. Elmer Merrill wrote in the 1943 edition of *Science* magazine. "The loss of the Berlin herbarium is a catastrophe of major proportions to world botany."

Directors of herbaria around the world are doing their best to retell the stories of their plant collections.

The largest herbaria in the world are located in the Museum of Natural History in Paris, the New York Botanical Garden, the Komarov Botanical Institute in St Petersburg, Russia, and the Royal Botanical Gardens at Kew. The herbarium at Kew, in west London, was started by the first Director of Kew Gardens, William Hooker, in his own home. Subsequent donations by eminent botanists meant that by 1877 there was a need for greater space. Yorkshireman Richard Spruce devoted his entire life to botanical explorations from the local Yorkshire flora to the Pyrenees and, at the request of William Hooker, he spent five years in the Amazon, Peru, and Ecuador, where he discovered the Cinchona plant—the source of quinine. Spruce suffered from extremely poor health, including intermittent bouts of malaria, and, on discovering the efficacy of the Cinchona on his symptoms, he sent seeds to India, where many thousands of lives were saved from the mosquito-transmitted killer disease. However, it is probable that Spruce benefited financially from this transaction and equally almost certain that the Ecuadoreans did not, so this is another example of the whole thorny question of biopiracy. Despite his ulterior financial motive, I can't help feeling fond of Spruce, who said in 1908: "I like to look on plants as sentient beings… which live and enjoy their lives…which beautify the earth and after death may adorn my herbarium…"

The herbarium at Kew has continued to grow—with new wings being added between 1903 and 1969, and then again in 1989, as more and more species flooded in from around the world. The collection now houses around seven million preserved specimens collected over 170 years, with around 25,000 more added each year. The modern wing that was incorporated in 2010 has climate control, which creates the perfect environment for keeping plants in optimum condition. Slowly the collection is being digitized and a database created so it can offer greater opportunities for research for anybody who needs it—from researchers in agriculture, environmental, and climate science to artists to scientists.

Then there is RHS Wisley, which contains over 90,000 ornamental plants out of a possible 400,000 grown in gardens in the UK today, and provides an essential resource for the ever-growing and popular RHS Plant Finder, which is an A–Z directory of plant names that also helpfully suggests where you can buy them.

Although the United States was a late starter in creating plant collections, it has certainly caught up, and in many places it has overtaken the rest of the world. Today, herbaria are generally accepted in the United States to be of national importance, and a knowledge of local plants is considered to be an essential part of a good education. The Americans have been particularly diligent about digitizing their specimens to allow greater access for botanists, climate scientists, and academic research. In February 2020, sixty-three million specimen records for plants and fungi were available online—most of these plants are held in US herbaria.

Today there are more than 3,300 herbaria in 178 countries holding nearly 390 million examples of plants gathered from the furthest corners of planet Earth. Little did the early collectors know how valuable their specimens would be to the future of botany, or that they would still be an essential resource for scientific study hundreds of years after they were first collected.

From the early collectors to the scientists who are digitizing the data for future scholars, it is impossible to name all the remarkable people who have collected, annotated, and cared for these collections. *Herbarium: The Quest to Preserve & Classify the World's Plants*, by Barbara M. Thiers, is an excellent reference for all things herbaria. To quote Thiers, herbaria are "a compelling reminder of one of humanity's better impulses: to save things—not just for ourselves, but for generations to come." It is also impossible to evaluate the enormous amount of time and trouble that has been taken to create these important records, which hold the key to many of the secrets of Earth and its survival.

Story

CARL LINNAEUS

Carl von Linné (1707–78) is the man who devised a standardized system for naming plants. Up until the time he set himself this massive task, the taxonomy of plants was rather haphazard, with the same plants being known by several different names in different parts of the world. Under his system, each plant was given two names (binomial); the first referred to the genus, the second to the species. For instance, *Rosa* (meaning rose) *canina* (meaning dog) is the Dog Rose. So passionate was he about the project that he even gave himself a binomial Latin name: "Carolus Linnaeus."

Nomenclature is the system of naming in a particular field or study. In his *Species Plantarum* of 1753, Carl Linnaeus set out a method for naming 7,300 plants, which was soon adopted by botanists the world over, and as a result he became known as the father of modern taxonomy. Linnaeus took a lot of names from the ancient Greek myths or the people who discovered them—such as *Rosa banksiae* after Joseph Banks.

Linnaeus was not the first to attempt to categorize plants. As far back as Theophrastus (370–287 CE) and Dioscorides (40–90 CE), scholars had been trying to create such a system. From mediaeval times the highly literate and educated Benedictine monks wrote down their knowledge of plants and their medicinal uses under their Latin names, but until the invention of the printing press, this information was only read by a few scholars. Linnaeus introduced order into a system that we still use to this day.

After he completed his magnum opus, *Species Plantarum*, Linnaeus went on to classify plants further according to the number of male and female reproductive organs they each had. In an attempt to make clear his findings about how plants reproduce, he used language that could be easily understood. By referring to the reproductive organs of plants with human names for male and female parts and sexual metaphors, he inadvertently created a botanical scandal. He describes the flower's petals as serving as "bridal beds." Explicit language and rather fanciful imaginings of the plants' sex lives were considered to be in very bad taste. In addition to what was generally quite shocking, the system did not really work as the basic premise was flawed. Darwin's Theory of Evolution had not yet been written, and Linnaeus had not understood that species could and would mutate over time.

After Linnaeus' death in 1778, his family sold his extensive collection of specimens and all his notebooks to James Edward Smith, who brought them to London and formed the Linnaean Society, which still exists today and is where botanists and interested parties meet to discuss new plant discoveries.

However, Carl Linnaeus leaves a great legacy. Plants are still named using his method, and any whose names were given to them by Linnaeus are correctly followed by the letter L—such as *Rosa Canina L.* His work lives on.

Caroli Linnæi
Medic: & Botan: Cult:
Stipend: Reg:
Præludia
Sponsaliorum
Plantarum
in quibus
Physiologia earum explicatur, Sexus demonstratur, modus generationis detegitur, nec non summa plantarum cum animalibus analogia concluditur

Upsal: 1729.

PRESSING FLOWERS

While the Victorians might have slipped a freshly picked flower between the pages of a book to preserve its beauty, we recommend using a flower press to get the best results. This device consists of two sturdy pieces of board (MDF works well) with layers of absorbent paper in between, screws through each corner and wing nuts to tighten. If you don't have one, though, a heavy book is still a serviceable tool for flower pressing.

We have found blotting paper to be most effective when pressing, as it does a very good job of drawing out moisture from the flowers quickly and efficiently, which is important to prevent them rotting. Most modern flower press sets will come complete with blotting paper and sheets of card to separate the layers, however, it is always good to have a few extra sheets to hand. The blotting paper absorbs moisture, while the card acts as a barrier, preventing the moisture bleeding into the next paper layer—so the thicker they are, the more effective they will be in the press. We source our blotting paper from John Purcell, a family-run business in South London that stocks every kind of paper you can imagine, and is a lovely excursion if you have a penchant for paper.

The process of pressing flowers is a slow one. It takes between one and four weeks to press a flower, depending on the type; for example, a wildflower with a tiny flower head and dainty stem will press in a few days, whereas a tulip may take several weeks to dry completely. So you must be patient. Switch off, take your time, and enjoy it.

SELECTING YOUR FLOWERS

When selecting flowers to press, make sure you choose specimens that have a beautiful shape. Look out for pretty wildflowers with windswept stems, or cut blooms from the garden that have twisted and turned to trap the sun's rays. If buying from your local florist or flower market, always choose seasonal varieties that catch your eye. Flowers with a flat petal structure and a slender stem will press best. Avoid flowers with large juicy heads, such as garden roses and peonies, because their petal structure is complex and will often result in mould forming in the press due to excess moisture that doesn't all escape.

The process of pressing flowers uses absorbent paper and pressure to draw all of the moisture out of the flower while flattening its form, so pick flowers when they are dry rather than after watering or a rain shower. The less moisture on the flowers when they go into the press, the quicker they will dry and the less chance there will be of mould forming.

Pick flowers at their peak, when they are standing tall with their petals unfurled. If cutting annuals, this process will have the same effect as deadheading—encouraging more and more flowers to grow. If you pick flowers that are already beginning to fade, they will only deteriorate further in the press, resulting in petals wrinkling at the edges or flower heads falling apart.

Plunge flowers into shallow water soon after cutting to keep them fresh. Pick some still in bud and arrange loosely in jars on the kitchen table, allowing them to come out over a couple of days for your own enjoyment before committing them to the press.

Aim to press your flowers on the same day as cutting or at the latest the day after you have picked them—certainly before they start to wilt—as this will give the blooms the best chance of retaining their colour and form.

1. Lay out your flowers, blotting the ends of the stems with an absorbent cloth to remove any moisture.

2. Start by laying down the bottom side of your flower press on a flat surface, feeding the screws up through the holes ready to slot over the top layer later. Position a sheet of card in the press, followed by a sheet of blotting paper. Place your first flower down in the middle of the blotting paper, trimming the stem if it is overlapping the edge of the paper. Leave plenty of room around the flower to allow the paper to absorb its moisture.

TIP: It is often easier to place the flowers face down to have more control over their positioning. Use your fingers to spread out the petals and leaves so they lie as flat as possible, taking care to arrange the flower in a naturalistic way. Be considerate here, and carefully arrange your plant specimens with precision. This initial placement plays an important role in the process of creating elegant and accurate pressed-flower compositions. You can edit at this stage. If any buds or leaves are hiding behind an open flower you can remove them by snipping with scissors. An unopened bud lying behind a flower head in the press can often cause bruising to the petals which will result in them turning brown.

3. Lay another sheet of blotting paper over the flower and press down gently. Place another layer of card on top, then another sheet of blotting paper.

TIP: As you press down on your first layer of paper, peel it back slightly to double check the petals are all lying flat, then unfold any that are not and check you are happy with the positioning before creating the next layer.

4. Lay down your next flower, alternating the placement of the flower heads on each layer to ensure an even distribution of moisture and thickness throughout the press. Make sure all stems and leaves are inside the paper layers and not sticking out of the sides of the press.

TIP: Multiple flower heads, stems, or complete specimens can be pressed in the same layer, as long as each one has its own space and stems aren't overlapping.

5. Repeat the same process until your press is full or you have used all of your blotting paper and card. Gently press down on the flower heads by hand as you add each paper layer, so your flowers don't bounce up and out as you build up the press.

6. After the last sheet of card, close your flower press by feeding the top of your flower press through the upright screws and pressing down firmly with one hand as you then screw it shut, tightening the wing nuts one by one until it feels secure and even. Store your press somewhere dry and warm and wait for five days before opening it. If the screws loosen during this time, press down again and tighten them up.

TIP: It's not necessary to store the press in an airing cupboard or specifically heated area, but do position it away from the cold. We stack ours on shelves on the warmest side of the studio, away from the windows.

OPENING YOUR PRESS

After five days, check your flowers. Open the press and carefully peel back each layer of paper, gently lifting the stems and petals. It's safer to peel the paper from the petals rather than the other way around, as petals can easily tear.

If the paper feels damp under the flower heads—which it often will, especially if the flower has a juicy centre—move the flower to the opposite side or, if very moist, replace with a fresh piece of blotting paper to prevent mould forming.

Close the press and leave for another five days before repeating this process, removing any flowers showing signs of mould so they don't contaminate the others. Regularly tighten the wing nuts, as they tend to loosen.

When the flowers feel papery to the touch and the stems are dry and brittle, they are ready to take out of the press. Depending on the types of flowers you have used, they should be fully dried and preserved after three to four weeks. Some flowers and plants will be ready in just a few days, such as delicate wildflowers, individual petals, leaves, or ferns.

We usually have lots of presses on the go, so we tend to organize our flowers by type, then group them in the press, as the same types will dry at a similar rate. Labelling the flowers in each press also helps you keep track. A strip of masking tape on the outside of the press marked with the flower and date of pressing does the job.

TIP: Your blotting paper and card can be reused again and again, just make sure the paper dries out completely between uses.

STORING YOUR FLOWERS

Flowers will be happy in the press until you need them, but if you need to use your press continuously throughout the seasons, pressed flowers can be stored safely elsewhere. We use mount board in various sizes to archive our flowers, fixing them in place with thin strips of masking tape over the stems. The boards are slipped into large plastic archive wallets and organized alphabetically in plan chests at the studio to keep them flat. You could also keep them in a drawer or storage box, separating them with layers of tissue paper—as long as they are kept dry and out of direct sunlight. As the flowers dry they become increasingly brittle and petals can curl, so it is important to keep them flat when storing for later use.

Story

SNOWDROP

The snowdrop in purest white array
First rears her head on Candlemas Day.
English folk lore

From the barren earth, a delicate little flower emerges, shivering in the frosty morning, speaking to us of hope and renewal. Then as the days begin to lengthen, the snowdrops gain momentum, pushing their impossibly fragile shoots through the iron earth.

The feast of Candlemas on 2 February is the snowdrop's due date. Their innocent demeanour, the bowed head, and tiny bell-like flowers, pure white with intricate green and sometimes yellow markings, associates them with purity and light after darkness, which is why they were often planted in graveyards and perhaps why they are also surrounded by superstition. Snowdrops can turn the milk, addle the eggs, and, to some gloomy souls, if they are brought over the threshold, they are harbingers of death.

Snowdrops are mountain flowers that were apparently brought to England by sixteenth-century monks, where they have naturalized and multiplied. The common snowdrop does not set seed but marches underground. In the garden they are the first flowers to arrive, and every year the little clumps grow larger and the return of this delicate little battalion is joyful. They also contain a substance called galantamine, which is helpful in the treatment of Alzheimer's disease. Facts like this stretch my mind. How do people find these things out? Scientists are wonderfully curious people.

The snowdrop's botanical name is *Galanthus nivalis*. It was named by Carl Linnaeus in 1735—from the Greek "*gala*" (meaning milk), "*anthos*" (meaning flower), and the Latin "*nivalis*" (of the snow). Snowdrop lovers are known as "galanthophiles" or, more unkindly, "galanthomaniacs," because some of the prices paid for a single snowdrop bulb seem almost incredible. In 2015 a galanthomaniac paid £1,390 on eBay for a single snowdrop bulb of *Galanthus plicatus* "Golden Fleece." This new strain took Joe Sharman of Monksilver Nursery over ten years to develop. Known affectionately as Mr Snowdrop, Joe is a member of a club of snowdrop enthusiasts who meet up to swap rare bulbs. As well as the swaps, he hunts for new hybrids in derelict Victorian gardens and private woodlands, where hybrids naturally occur, then cultivates them. When you understand that it took Joe six years to propagate 100 bulbs of *Galanthus plicatus* "E. A. Bowles"—discovered in Myddelton House, in Enfield, London, in 2004—from the single bulb he was gifted, it goes some way to help us understand why they command such high prices. The snowdrop enthusiast's passion for developing new strains brings its own problems, because there are plenty of people who will go to great lengths to

get their hands on one. In England in 2019, two men were jailed for stealing 13,000 bulbs in a nocturnal raid in the grounds of Walsingham Abbey, in Norfolk, which had a "street value" of around £1,500.

Stealing rare snowdrops, however, is as complicated as stealing a painting by a well-known artist. The minute you put the bulbs up for sale, galanthophiles know exactly who propagated the plant and where it was stolen from, so you have to know who you are going to sell to before you pinch it. The galanthophiles go to great trouble to keep their new hybrids secret; they will not let strangers into their gardens or nurseries and will even take the heads off flowers to stop people recognizing them. They always give one bulb away to a friend for security, too, so they can start again if necessary. This passion, bordering on obsession, seems unlikely for such a modest little flower.

Unsurprisingly, many of the stories that have arisen around the snowdrop are to do with its early arrival at the start of the new year. In the Russian folk tale "The Twelve Months," by Samuil Marshak, a little girl is sent by her wicked stepmother and ugly stepsister (sound familiar?) to find spring flowers in the forest to please a capricious and ignorant queen. The weather is appalling and the child is in danger of dying on her hopeless quest. She is saved by meeting twelve brothers, who each represent the months of the year, sitting round a fire in the forest. They take pity on her, and using their powers they bring her magical snowdrops in January, which she gathers and takes home to her ungrateful family. In the end, of course, the good little girl is fine and the wicked relatives get their comeuppance. There are many versions of this story, and two films have also been made, including a Russian animated film in 1956 and a Japanese cartoon in 1980—which you can watch on YouTube.

Pressed flowers are haunting little fragile things that evoke memory and sentiment.

I particularly like the story of "The Snowdrop" by Hans Christian Andersen, because it has a pressed flower at the centre of it. It is the tale of an intrepid little snowdrop who insists on coming out too soon. Her beauty is great and unexpected in the forest, where everything else seems dead and bleak. An observant little girl sees the tiny flower and is awestruck by its delicacy and loveliness. She picks it, then takes it home and presses it between the leaves of a book. Several years later, she gives the snowdrop as a love token to a young man, along with a poem. The poem and the snowdrop are kept by him tenderly, together with her letters. When the young man discovers that she has betrayed him, he bitterly casts the love letters and poetry into the fire, but the pressed snowdrop falls to the ground unnoticed, where it is discovered by a servant. There is something about the little flattened snowdrop carelessly cast aside that touches the servant and she slips it into another book of poetry. There it lies, preserved and undiscovered, for many years until a scholar finds it and he is moved by it, imagining that the flower must have meant something to somebody once, and so he leaves it there. Pressed flowers are like that, haunting little fragile things that evoke memory and sentiment.

Snowdrops are so white that they can be seen even on a moonless night, which is why they were often planted to guide the way to a doorway or an outside privy. They appear from the dark earth when the winter is at its absolute bleakest and it feels like all hope is gone. When we creep out of bed in the darkness and slope off to the market with bad grace—we can't imagine why we ever decided to be florists at all, what with the early mornings and the biting cold—the sight of the snowdrops lifts our spirits. We cut one or two from each clump and open the presses…

Musing

PRESSING WILDFLOWERS

Contrary to popular belief, it is not always illegal to pick all wildflowers, in fact, for some plants it can actually be beneficial for them. By removing a few flowers you encourage the plant to produce more blooms, and disturbing the seedheads allows the seeds to fall to the ground, so they can reproduce and reappear the following year. However, it is important to know what you can and cannot pick when setting out to find a few wildflowers to press. Here are a few tips to help you make the right decisions.

1. Do not pick endangered or protected flowers. In the UK, there is a list that you can find within The Wildlife and Countryside Act, Section 8, or in the US, check with the Endangered Species list from the Fish and Wildlife Services (FSA) Take a book of wildflowers with you and try to identify the species before picking; if you are not certain, leave them alone.
2. Pick only one flower in twenty. If there are fewer than twenty blooms in the area you are picking from, move on until you find more.
3. Leave plenty of flowers for others to enjoy.
4. Never pull up wildflowers by the roots. Leave the majority of the plant untouched so it can continue to thrive. Just cut the flowers by the stem—use scissors, don't yank at them. It is fine to take a bit of foliage too, but leave plenty so the plant can continue to photosynthesize.
5. Do not pick flowers from private land without the express permission of the land owners.
6. Do not pick flowers from parks, people's front gardens, or from roundabouts.

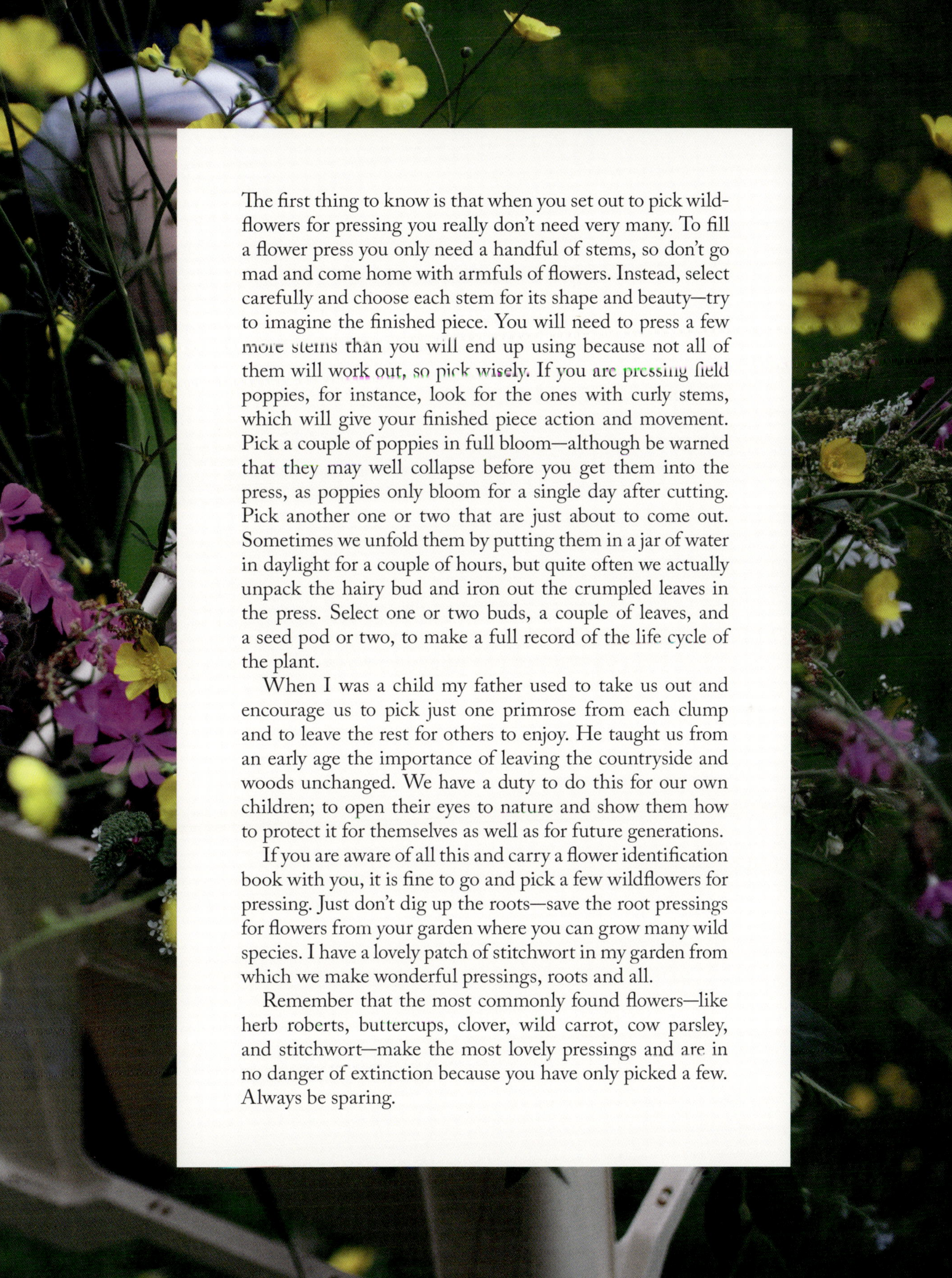

The first thing to know is that when you set out to pick wildflowers for pressing you really don't need very many. To fill a flower press you only need a handful of stems, so don't go mad and come home with armfuls of flowers. Instead, select carefully and choose each stem for its shape and beauty—try to imagine the finished piece. You will need to press a few more stems than you will end up using because not all of them will work out, so pick wisely. If you are pressing field poppies, for instance, look for the ones with curly stems, which will give your finished piece action and movement. Pick a couple of poppies in full bloom—although be warned that they may well collapse before you get them into the press, as poppies only bloom for a single day after cutting. Pick another one or two that are just about to come out. Sometimes we unfold them by putting them in a jar of water in daylight for a couple of hours, but quite often we actually unpack the hairy bud and iron out the crumpled leaves in the press. Select one or two buds, a couple of leaves, and a seed pod or two, to make a full record of the life cycle of the plant.

When I was a child my father used to take us out and encourage us to pick just one primrose from each clump and to leave the rest for others to enjoy. He taught us from an early age the importance of leaving the countryside and woods unchanged. We have a duty to do this for our own children; to open their eyes to nature and show them how to protect it for themselves as well as for future generations.

If you are aware of all this and carry a flower identification book with you, it is fine to go and pick a few wildflowers for pressing. Just don't dig up the roots—save the root pressings for flowers from your garden where you can grow many wild species. I have a lovely patch of stitchwort in my garden from which we make wonderful pressings, roots and all.

Remember that the most commonly found flowers—like herb roberts, buttercups, clover, wild carrot, cow parsley, and stitchwort—make the most lovely pressings and are in no danger of extinction because you have only picked a few. Always be sparing.

Story

NARCISSUS

I wandered lonely as a cloud
That floats on high o'er vales and hills,
When all at once I saw a crowd,
A host, of golden daffodils;
Beside the lake, beneath the trees,
Fluttering and dancing in the breeze.
"I Wandered Lonely as a Cloud," William Wordsworth (1770–1850)

"I see the daffodils have come up yellow again," said my friend, all world-weary on the telephone. William Wordsworth was much more excited when he came upon thousands of wild daffodils "fluttering and dancing in the breeze" while walking in the hills above Grasmere, in the Lake District.

There is something very reassuring about the annual recurrence of daffodils in parks, woods, meadows and grassy verges, on hillsides, and in our own gardens. They appear at the end of the long, dark winter, their little trumpets cheerfully heralding the arrival of spring.

When I was a tiny child we moved to Long House, in Sussex, where my father planted thousands of daffodils down the drive and in the orchards of the gardens, which had long been deserted before he came to rescue them. The first glorious burst of sunshine brought the flowers out almost overnight

so that suddenly the garden was filled with joy. The long, cold winter was over and spring turned into an endless summer. There were so many we were allowed to pick them and bring them to my mother, clasped in our hot little hands with the sap seeping like saliva from the bright green stems. When we were children, time was elastic and stretched interminably. Nowadays the seasons go past in a flash, easy to miss altogether if you are staring at your computer screen. Growing flowers is a good way to record the passage of time. Start with a few daffodil bulbs, why not? They are easy to grow and wonderfully reliable. My two favourites are "Cheerfulness" and also "Poeticus," otherwise known as "Pheasant's Eye."

Great boxes arrive from the Scilly Isles, off the southwest coast of England, at New Covent Garden Flower Market in early spring—in a hundred shades of yellow, cream, and orange—smelling sweetly of hope and the promise of more light.

A surprise gleaned while researching for this book was that *Narcissus* is a genus of spring-flowering, perennial plants of the amaryllis family. Further investigation revealed that its various common names include daffodil, narcissus, and jonquil. Despite what florists and gardeners may tell you, there is no difference in the genus, although there are thousands of different cultivars. I always thought that narcissi were the little multi-headed ones and daffodils were the big ones, but no—daffodils, narcissi, they are one and the same. You are always learning something new in the floristry game.

Pressing narcissi is certainly possible, but it's not a good flower to start with. At JamJar we first attempted the process for a publicity launch of a daffodil-inspired fragrance called Ostara for Penhaligon's—a lovely, traditional, British perfume company. The plan was to send journalists jam jars full of fresh daffodils delivered on bicycles by handsome male models, along with a charming little yellow notebook with a few pressed flowers inside.

This was very early in our pressing experience and it was, frankly, a disaster. We prepared hundreds of fat yellow daffodils, but when we opened the presses we found the swollen ovaries at the base of the flowers had just pulped into a mouldy mess. We were running out of time and dashed to the market to buy the tiny little variety, "Tête-à-Tête." The deadline was closing in and they just weren't drying fast enough. We opened and closed the enormous book press we were using and gloomily observed that the flowers still looked worryingly juicy.

Eventually, in a fit of panic, I took home several hundred flowers between sheets of blotting paper and put them in the oven at a a low temperature. Cue my husband, who always does everything at the rate of knots, dashing home, turning the oven on full, with fan, ready to make dinner. Cut to my scream, "NOOOO!" and I opened the oven door to thousands of tiny, half-pressed "Tête-à-Têtes" flying up into the kitchen in a hot yellow tornado.

In the end we got them pressed. I even think an iron was used at one point (not recommended). We are better than this now. Note to fashion and beauty companies: If you want a project executed beautifully, and if you want to use pressed flowers, give us a long lead-in. Some things just can't be rushed.

There are some beautiful myths about how narcissus got its name. Here is my favourite and the most famous as told by the Roman poet, Ovid: Narcissus was a golden boy from Ancient Greece, who was extraordinarily beautiful. A mountain nymph called Echo saw him walking in the woods and was entranced. Echo had been punished for offending the goddess Hera, who deprived her of speech, and so she could only repeat the last words she heard. She followed Narcissus, who could feel her presence but could not see her. He called out, "Who is there?" Poor Echo could only return the plaintive cry, "Who is there?"

This was obviously annoying, so when she eventually revealed herself and tried to embrace Narcissus, he turned from her in disdain. Rejection devastated the nymph. Echo remained obsessed with Narcissus and she retreated into the wild valleys where she wandered, repeating her mournful cry, until she became a wraith and perished. All that was left of her was the echo.

Nemesis, the goddess of revenge (who is Aphrodite in disguise), saw this and decided to punish Narcissus. She lured him to a pool of perfectly still water and, as he leaned over to drink, he was transfixed by the first sight of his own beautiful reflection. Unable to tear himself away, he fell in love as hopelessly as Echo had done before him. Perhaps he wasn't very bright, for it took a while, but eventually it dawned on him that every time he reached for the object of his desire the water broke up and the image disappeared. Nothing could ever come of this futile love that burned him up, but still he could not leave. He was consumed by his narcissism.

Some versions of the story have it that he killed himself, others that he merely wasted away beside the water. In all of these, though, he turns into the fragrant, white and golden flower that is named after him.

The term "narcissism" was first coined in 1899 by Havelock Ellis, a prudish, Victorian sexologist who used it to describe a predilection for masturbation. In 1911, Otto Rank used the term to describe excessive vanity, and in 1914 Sigmund Freud confirmed the term into the psychological vernacular by publishing a paper called "On Narcissism: An introduction."

One of my favourite literary descriptions of a narcissist is Oscar Wilde's novella *The Picture of Dorian Gray*, the sinister story of a beautiful man whose behaviour becomes more and more loathsome although his beauty remains flawless—"beautiful inside and out" he certainly is not. Only Dorian knows what is happening to the portrait in the attic. If you haven't read it, I can highly recommend it. More recently, Narcissa Malfoy, the self-obsessed, pure-blooded, dark witch in the *Harry Potter* series, is named for the myth.

It is interesting to consider that, for the past 2,000 years, narcissism has been considered generally to be a bad thing from which no good can come (well, with the exception of beautiful flowers). I remember my children's grandmother complimenting me on their looks *in French*. I asked her why we were suddenly speaking French. She said she didn't want the children to get "swollen-headed." They were two and four at the time.

Before we started JamJar Flowers, I ran a successful London modelling agency for twenty-seven years. When we opened the agency in 1982, even the most ravishing creatures constantly underplayed their looks as it was considered hugely unattractive to put yourself forward—or to be seen to be vain. The boys, in particular, seemed to be almost deliberately unkempt, sometimes actually dirty. The girls often wore no makeup and just let their lovely faces do the work for them. If you told them how beautiful they were, they smiled shyly and made some disparaging remark.

Recently, however, there has been a seismic shift in our perception of vanity. Since the invention of social media, particularly Instagram, it seems to be something to be celebrated, almost as a necessity. We are endlessly encouraged to put up flattering photographs of ourselves to which people largely respond with dazzling praise, swoons, hearts, and fiery emojis.

Recently, I visited the Taj Mahal for the first time. Despite all the many, many images we had seen before, we were not remotely prepared for the way the breath was sucked out of our bodies as the exquisite mausoleum was revealed. The great mass of pure white marble seems to hover above the ground, weightless and ethereal, in the shimmering, dusty Indian light. It was definitely strange, at this moment, to find ourselves faced with masses of tourists with their backs to the building, selfie sticks aloft, ruining that perfect symmetry to capture their own image squarely in the middle of the frame. This seems to be an entirely modern phenomenon as we spin our smartphone cameras around to photograph ourselves. I do think that the young Narcissus would have approved, though.

Project

FRITILLARIES

One April, Amy, our colleague India, and I headed to Thyme, in Gloucestershire, for a working holiday. We were making the finishing touches to the text for this book as well as collecting flowers to press for an exhibition that would be held at Thyme during the summer. We wanted the flowers we used to reflect what was growing in the area immediately around the estate.

To say it was not a warm spring is an understatement; the weather was freezing as we stamped out of our cozy cottage across the squelchy water meadows looking for flowers to press. After a while your eye gets accustomed to scanning the hedgerows for jewels, and we found wood anemones, dog vio-

lets, primroses, cowslips, daisies, and early bluebells. Then on our way home, with our baskets full, we came across the most lovely sight under a giant oak tree—a whole host of fritillaries growing in a magic circle. The delicate little flowers danced in the breeze, twisting and curling with their snakelike heads and amazing chequered markings. We gathered lots for pressing and picked a few of the grasses that grew among them. We were on private land with permission to gather the flowers, but even so, we picked so carefully that we made no impact on the beautiful scene.

To replicate our view that afternoon, we arranged fritillaries and grasses in a wide, landscape composition to hang in the barn long after the fritillaries had died back. The most successful compositions are often the simplest. The Edwardian ladies who made complicated fantasy flowers by cobbling together different species, in our opinion, lost the beauty of nature. Perhaps it doesn't need to be improved upon. Perhaps it cannot be improved on.

MOUNTING PRESSED FLOWERS

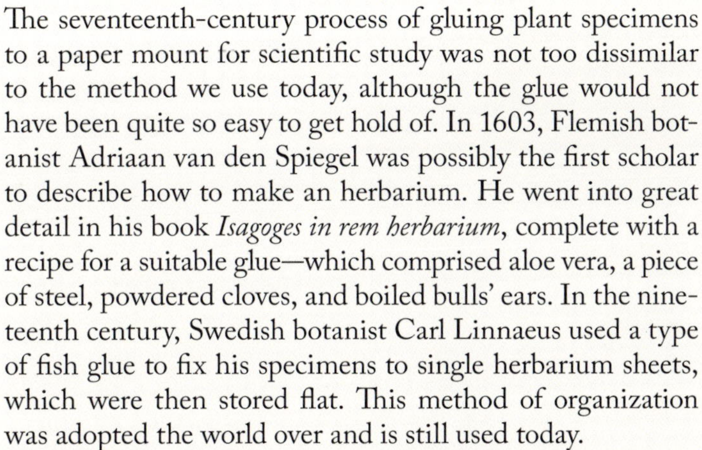

The seventeenth-century process of gluing plant specimens to a paper mount for scientific study was not too dissimilar to the method we use today, although the glue would not have been quite so easy to get hold of. In 1603, Flemish botanist Adriaan van den Spiegel was possibly the first scholar to describe how to make an herbarium. He went into great detail in his book *Isagoges in rem herbarium*, complete with a recipe for a suitable glue—which comprised aloe vera, a piece of steel, powdered cloves, and boiled bulls' ears. In the nineteenth century, Swedish botanist Carl Linnaeus used a type of fish glue to fix his specimens to single herbarium sheets, which were then stored flat. This method of organization was adopted the world over and is still used today.

Things have moved on from boiled bulls' ears, and we recommend using a gentle water-based and acid-free glue to secure your flowers to your chosen surface. We tried everything from PVA to a fine Japanese rice glue, but then eventually we found the most user-friendly glue was Mod Podge, which falls somewhere in between. Mod Podge is a water-based sealant, glue, and finish that dries to the touch in twenty to thirty minutes and is available from most art supply stores. We have used this glue on all of the pressed flower projects we mention in this book. So, here's how we go about mounting pressed flowers.

TOOLS

Water-based, acid-free glue
Selection of small paintbrushes
Scrap card or paper
Tweezers
Pins, or any other small item to use as markers
Acid-free mount board, cotton rag, paper, or your surface of choice

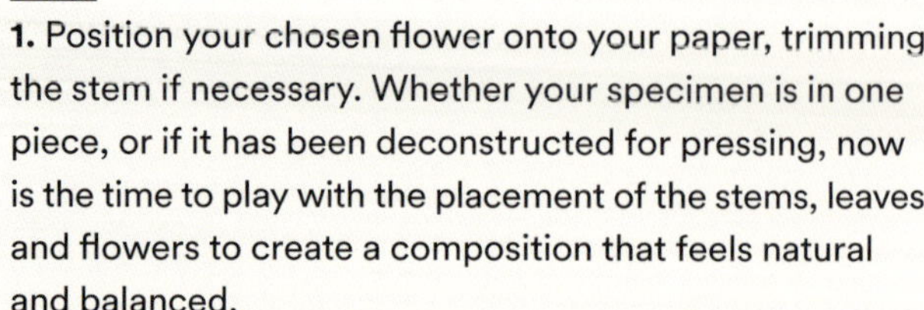

1. Position your chosen flower onto your paper, trimming the stem if necessary. Whether your specimen is in one piece, or if it has been deconstructed for pressing, now is the time to play with the placement of the stems, leaves and flowers to create a composition that feels natural and balanced.

TIP: Think about how the flower would grow naturally when constructing your composition. We like to leave plenty of space around each one to allow them to speak for themselves. We add extra stems, buds, or flower heads to create fuller compositions with movement and shape, making sure all the separate parts come from the same species, if not the same specimen.

2. Once you are happy with the positioning, place several pins or markers on the paper at the tips of the flower heads, stems, and leaves as a reminder of where to place the specimen while you apply the glue.

3. Place your flower face down on a scrap piece of card or paper. Using a very small paintbrush, apply a thin, even layer of glue over the specimen, starting with the stem and leaves. You need to work quickly but carefully, taking extra care when brushing the brittle leaves. To apply glue to the flower head, brush gently from the centre of the flower outwards if the petals feel secure; don't apply glue directly to petals that feel fragile.

TIP: It can be safer to roll the brush from the centre of the flower out towards the edge of the petals, as brushing can drag on delicate petals, causing them to dislodge or tear. You may wish to leave a blob of glue on the back of the flower head and secure the petals later if they're too delicate—we do this with poppies.

4. With your fingers or tweezers, gently lift the specimen from the card by the stem, flip over, and hold above your chosen surface. Use the other end of your paintbrush or a pencil to support any floppy or bending stems. Gently lower into position, starting with the stem and fixing it down all the way to the flower heads, then press down gently with your fingertips.

5. If you have not glued your petals, lift them carefully with tweezers or a pin and paint a thin layer of glue directly onto the paper or surface where you want them to rest. Press down gently and repeat all the way around the flower head until all of the petals are secured.

TIP: Try to glue down as much of the surface of the specimen as you can. Too little glue and the edges of the leaves and petals can crinkle. But be careful not to over-apply, as too much glue will seep out of the sides. If this happens, use a slightly damp cloth to gently dab away the excess. Give the pressing a gentle blow to see if any parts or petals are loose.

6. Once glued, cover the specimen with a clean sheet of paper, or greaseproof or wax paper if you have it, and weigh down with a heavy book or stack of magazines for a few hours or overnight until the glue has dried. Clean brushes with soap and water after use.

Story

BLUEBELL

If you enter an English bluebell wood at dawn or dusk it is easy to believe in magic. In folklore, the flower's bells ring to summon the little folk to gatherings. If you, a human being, have heard the bluebells chime, you are not long for this world; the deep magic is always a little bit sinister, and faeries are not always good.

On an English late-spring day, when the sun is high and the skylarks are singing, it can look as if the sky fell down onto the forest's ferny floor. Thousands and thousands of bluebells stretch your gaze to the horizon and a poignant fragrance hangs in the air. With their arching backs and beautiful little bells all hung down one side of the flower, you wonder how on earth these millions of plants spread out before you could be endangered? And yet they are. The English bluebells (*Hyacinthoides non-scripta*) are being invaded by their Spanish cousins (*Hyacinthoides hispanica*), who will overtake them by hybridizing, and the stronger species will eventually wipe out the "*non scripta*" if we are not very careful. I have seen them growing side by side in the woods, but it could have been *Hyacinthoides* x *massartiana*, a half-breed offspring of the two species. Like everything else in nature, eventually the stronger species will prevail without the careful intervention of man, who probably introduced the rogue species, in all innocence, in the first place.

"*Non scripta*" means simply "unwritten," which already sounds a little ominous. We cannot lose this most English of flowers. That flash of blue, sighted from the car as we whizz about on our journeys, stops us in our tracks and causes us to slow down, park up, and enter into the ancient enchanted woodland. But stick to the paths, as crushing the leaves prevents photosynthesis and kills the plant, and also old folklore predicts terrible bad luck coming to the people who trample bluebells in the woods, and those who pick the flowers and bring them into their homes. These stories have been useful, though, because they protected the bluebell from loss of habitat, and it can take years for them to recover after being carelessly walked over in the woods.

Bluebells attract woodland butterflies, bees, and hoverflies, which all feed on their nectar. Lazy bees sometimes bite the bottom of the flower to steal the nectar without bothering to squeeze inside the tubular bells and do their job of pollinating the plants, but the bluebell can reproduce asexually by bulb division as well as by pollination.

The bluebell, as the Latin name suggests, is part of the hyacinth family, which is a sub-division of the asparagus family. Hyacinthus, after whom they are named, was an athletic Spartan youth of extraordinary beauty, beloved by the god Apollo. Together they hunted and climbed, made love and beautiful music, and visited Apollo's kingdom in a chariot drawn by swans. One day, while sporting with his lover, Apollo threw the discus so high that it

Bluebell

"scattered the clouds," according to Ovid, then fell to the earth, striking Hyacinthus on the back of the head and instantly killing him. Apollo was devastated, and there are many depictions of him holding his darling boy in his arms. He wanted to die of grief himself, but instead he caused the flower to grow where Hyacinthus fell and wrote "*ai ai*" (alas, alas) on its petals.

The English bluebell is not to be confused with the harebell (*Campanula rotundifolia*), which is confusingly called bluebell in Scotland. The lovely old tune "The Bluebells of Scotland" is actually a song about harebells, which are equally as blue but a completely different flower and genus. Bluebells have very toxic bulbs and a gummy sap that, in Elizabethan times, was used to starch the fashionable pleated ruffs and to set the tail feathers onto arrows. The poisonous sap was also used for bookbinding, as it stopped bugs from eating and destroying the books. Monks in the thirteenth century used bluebells to cure snake and spider bites, leprosy, and tuberculosis. Given the toxic nature of the plant this seems like a kill or cure method that can have been only partially successful.

There is a lot of misunderstanding around the level of protection for bluebells. It is not actually illegal to pick the flower of an English bluebell, but it is forbidden to uproot the bulbs and remove them from the soil, even if you own the land, as it takes about five years for a bluebell to grow from seed to bulb. There are unscrupulous people who will steal bulbs to sell to garden centres, so it is now illegal to trade in *Hyacinthoides non-scripta* seeds or bulbs. Although, I noticed when looking them up that there are many garden centres that still seem to be offering the bulbs for sale. I am sure there is a perfectly legitimate explanation for them being on offer, but please don't buy them, as by proving there is a market you will only increase the temptation for people to dig them up.

A bluebell is not worth picking, as it dies very quickly in a jar of water.

As a child I remember my father grinding the car to a halt and leaping out to shout at some terrified townies who had come down to the countryside to picnic in the woods. They had picked armfuls of bluebells and laid them out carefully in the boot of their car. We sat open-mouthed, with our noses pressed up against the car window, as our handsome father told them what was what: "You bloody fools, what do you think you are doing? You are destroying the countryside and these flowers will be dead by the time you get them back to London. Look, look, these are the roots you have pulled up. This little white bulb is the future of the plant. You are not just destroying the place for this year, but forever!" We sank back in our seats, awestruck and feeling more than a little sorry for the harassed-looking sinners. But he was right, a bluebell is not really worth picking, as it dies very quickly in a jar of water. It is best left to be enjoyed in carpets in ancient woodlands.

For these reasons of preservation we use the Spanish bluebell for pressing, which arrives without invitation in my garden. It is not, in my opinion, as lovely as the delicate English bluebell—it has a straight stem and the blooms appear on both sides—but it still makes a lovely pressed flower.

Guide

DECORATIVE TILES

I have always used attractive tiles I've picked up on holidays in Portugal and Morocco as placemats. Amy sourced these lovely ceramic ones at her local tile shop, and we like their rustic simplicity. My absolute favourite, the little violet with roots, lost all its colour when we applied glue over it, but white violets are very beautiful and desirable—and, as always, it is more about their shape than their colour. I love all four of these tiles. I kept them on the basin in my downstairs bathroom for a while as a splashback, and grew very attached to them, but Amy suggested we should bring them into the studio and test them with hot coffee cups so we could see how they performed under heat. The experiment is ongoing, but so far so good—they are holding up brilliantly.

PREPARE THE TILE SURFACE

Wipe away any dust on the tile surface and apply a layer of glue in matte finish with a clean brush. This will seal the top of the tile and give you a nice even surface onto which to apply the flowers. Allow to dry thoroughly.

POSITION YOUR FLOWERS

Lay out the flowers and cut the stems to size, allowing plenty of space around the edges for an attractive composition. Choose flowers with flat stems for an even surface if you plan to use the tiles as coasters. Add leaves or buds to bare stems for more interest. Apply a thin layer of glue to the back of each flower, over the whole surface. If the petals are too delicate, only apply glue to the stem, then apply it directly to the tile under the flower head. Press down and leave to dry.

APPLY SEALANT

Once dry, paint over the flower and entire surface of the tile with more glue. Apply three or four coats, allowing to dry completely in between each coat. Once dry, apply a layer of sealant—we used PlastiKote spray sealant with a matte finish—or use clear varnish or resin for a hardier topcoat.

Story

PRIMULA

Where the bee sucks, there suck I:
In a cowslip's bell I lie;
There I couch when owls do cry.
On the bat's back I do fly.
The Tempest, William Shakespeare (1564–1616)

The name "Primrose" (*Primula vulgaris*) is a corruption of "Prima Rosa," the first rose or the first flower. Of course, it isn't a rose, or indeed the first flower, but when you see the buttery clumps of primrose in the hedgerows, or on the banks of a stream, you know that spring has really arrived. Their pretty, pale faces with a bright orange eye, slender hairy stems, and thick, crinkly, green leaves make the most attractive posies for the wildflower gatherer.

In Shakespeare's *Macbeth*, the drunken porter describes the road to hell as: "The primrose path to the everlasting bonfire," implying that the road to righteousness should be a difficult one. What could be more agreeable or seemingly more innocent than treading a path lined with primroses?

The primula has many forms, one of my favourites being the cowslip (*Primula veris*), a cheerful little variant of *Primula vulgaris*. The familiar name comes from their growing where the cows slop, apparently. Unlike its cousin the primrose, the cowslip has many tiny florets on a single stem. It is supposed to resemble a bunch of keys, and in the Middle Ages it was known by monks as St Peter's herb. Allegedly, St Peter carelessly dropped the keys to the gates of Heaven and all a sinner needs is a cowslip to get past him when he isn't looking.

Until recently, cowslips were losing habitat at a frightening speed, but since the practice of spraying hedgerows and verges has largely ceased, it is making up for lost time and spreading itself cheerfully about. The very similar-looking, but much rarer, oxlip (*Primula elatior*) has not had so much luck and is now found mainly in East Anglia, where it still has a foothold. The fashion for wildflower meadows has also greatly increased cowslip numbers.

One of my favourite Beatrix Potter illustrations is of Cecily Parker (an adorable rabbit in sprigged muslin) making cowslip wine. Originally Cecily was making cider, but Potter's publishers, Warne, decided that children's books should not have alcohol in them—even though there are, in fact, many recipes for cowslip wine today and all of them are quite alcoholic.

Polyanthus (*Primula* x *polyantha*), meaning literally "many flowers," is a garden variety of the primrose, usually distinguished by having many florets at the end of a single stem. It is a very popular garden plant, coming in myriad brilliant colours, covering the whole spectrum from white to a deep indigo. Keep deadheading and you will have their bright little faces to enjoy when there is little else in the garden.

The diva of the primula species is, without a doubt, the auricula (*Primula auricula*)—my favourite. Although auriculas have been around since Elizabethan times, they did not really gain popularity in the UK until the arrival of the Huguenots in the seventeenth century, who were escaping religious persecution in France. These silk weavers arrived in Spitalfields, in East London, where they built the most beautiful houses, bringing with them seeds of auricula. The Huguenots were enthusiastic botanists and in the small backyards of their lovely houses, and then on allotments on the edge of town, they grew plants for competitions and "Florists Feasts"—precursors of today's horticultural shows—where people came to enjoy the flowers, then have a festive meal. The Huguenots coined the name "Florist" for flower specialists. They brought their love of flowers to the East End of London, starting a flower market in Bethnal Green, which is thought to be the origins of today's thriving Columbia Road Market.

The auricula is an exquisite little flower of such intricacy, variation, and beauty that it has been celebrated by gardeners and artists alike for many centuries. It is an alpine whose original habitat was in the rock fissures of the European alps, so cold and frost do not bother them, but, according to auricula specialist Robin Graham: "They don't like sunbathing or swimming."

Some genius worked out that the best way to display the extraordinary qualities of this lovely plant and its endless variety was in an auricula theatre, where the plants are displayed in serried ranks, normally against a black background—although sometimes a particularly special one is framed in gold. I fell in love with these displays a decade ago at the Chelsea Flower Show, where one by the modestly named gold-medallist Pop's Plants quite took my breath away.

In Victorian times many of the great gardens had an auricula theatre. Sometimes each individual plant was brought out from behind a curtain and placed on a stand where the audience, seated on chairs, could sit and admire the spectacle. Each individual flower would receive a round of applause, then be removed from sight to await the finale, when the curtain was drawn back and all the stars would be viewed together. "The perfection of a stage auricula is that of the most exquisite Meissen porcelain or of the most lovely silk stuffs of Isfahan and yet it is a living growing thing," said the writer, critic, and aesthete Sacheverell Sitwell (1897–1988), brother to Osbert and the redoubtable Dame Edith. The most famous auricula theatre still in existence is at Calke Abbey, in Derbyshire, where the plants are displayed on a specially built raked stage.

The auricula is a specialist's plant, an obsessive collector's plant.

But oh, these plants are so difficult to grow. After seeing the Pop's Plants display at Chelsea, I bought a small theatre and thirty different auricula plugs for my sister Vicky and her husband Anthony, for their wedding anniversary. They are both wonderful gardeners and I thought it was the best present ever. But it turned out to be a bit of a loaded gift. The plants just didn't thrive in their garden, despite their very best efforts. In the end we opted for the more easily grown primula, "Gold-Laced Group," which is a lovely plant, but it doesn't have the exceptional qualities of an auricula.

The auricula is a specialist's plant, an obsessive collector's plant, for people who suffer from a rare disease called auriculitis. It is not for the casual gardener. There is too much room for disappointment.

Story

VIOLET

If you forget me, think
Of our gifts to Aphrodite
And all the loveliness that we shared
–
All the violet tiaras,
Braided rosebuds, dill and
Crocus twined around your young neck
–
Myrrh poured on your head
And on soft mats girls with
All that they most wished for beside them.

"No Word," Sappho (630–570 BCE)

If you're not looking for wild violets on the edge of a wood, they're easily missed, for they are humble flowers that creep just above the ground. *Viola odorata* grows in small clumps, and has an exquisite beauty and a sweet scent. More commonly found in the wild is the dog violet—equally precious as its fragrant cousin *Viola odorata*, but it doesn't have a scent. These violets are the smallest genus from the family Violaceae—the viola is its larger cousin, and the pansy is the flashy film star of the family.

When I was a child my mother used to send us out to look for *Viola odorata*. There was a modest prize for the first child to bring one home—a good way to occupy bored children living deep in the countryside! For this reason, perhaps, I have always thought of violets as a rare and precious flower.

I'm not alone. Violets have been highly prized for millennia because of their delicious fragrance, which was the basis for many perfumes. Today, very few scent manufacturers actually use violet flower extract as a base for their fragrances (you can imagine how many tiny blooms you would need to harvest to make any kind of significant extraction), but the violet leaf is still used in perfumery to this day.

Essence of violet was commonly used in confectionery and to flavour sweet treats. My children's great-grandmother had a great love for rose and violet creams, the most regal chocolates made by Royal Appointment to Her Majesty the Queen, who, presumably, is fond of them too. Each dark chocolate has a creamy centre flavoured with essence of rose or violet and a crystallized flower or petal on top. When I was a child there was a particularly disgusting candy called Parma Violets, which were a sickly lavender colour and tasted strongly, and nastily, of soap. I doubt their particularly noxious taste had anything much to do with the flower, but the memory lingers.

The leaves of the violet are edible and can be used in salads; while the floral extract is used as a culinary flavouring in many European countries. Like rosewater, it is important not to use too much—a few drops go a long way. Violets are also still used in a number of herbal medicines for treating respiratory ailments, insomnia and some skin disorders.

If you encourage a violet into your garden—as I did with the adorable *Viola labradorica*, with its almost black leaves and minute, deep-purple flowers—you'll discover it is a pervasive invader. I spend as much time yanking it out of the gravel as I do admiring it in its brief flowering period. I was pleased to find that Prince Charles had the same problem when I visited the gift shop in his magnificent gardens at Highgrove. *Viola labradorica* were underfoot everywhere, invading the gravel.

The flowers were worn by Victorian ladies as a nosegay, or a buttonhole. Small bunches, surrounded by their own leaves, were made up by the flower girls in Covent Garden market. Like Eliza Doolittle in *My Fair Lady*, they carried big baskets of amethyst-coloured violets to sell to young men in the early morning. More beautiful, and certainly more affordable, than any jewel, they were given as tokens of love.

Violets have also long been associated with lesbians, after Sappho, the Greek poet, wrote tenderly of her lover wearing a garland of violets, and in 1926 a play called *La Prisonnière (The Captive)* by Edouard Bourdet used the gift of a bunch of violets to symbolize lesbian love. By the mid-twentieth century, violets were given by women to other women as a symbol of their intent and sexual preference.

As well as a token of love, violets are apparently helpful in the breakup of a relationship. Steep violets in hot water and drink the tea and your heartbreak will be cured, or it may at the very least send you to sleep so that you stop thinking about it.

Shakespeare was very fond of violets; referring to them often in his plays by their lovely familiar name of "love in idleness." In Act 2, Scene 1 of *A Midsummer Night's Dream*, under the instruction of the faerie king Oberon, Puck makes a love potion out of violets and squeezes it onto the eyelids of his sleeping queen, Titania, tricking her into falling in love with Bottom the weaver with his ass's head on. Then in his tragedy *Hamlet*, the eponymous hero is unfaithful to Ophelia, and withering violets symbolize his betrayal. Mourning at her graveside in Act 5, Scene 1, her father, Laertes, says:

> Lay her i' th' earth,
> And from her fair and unpolluted flesh
> May violets spring!

This image endured. In the ravishing Pre-Raphaelite painting of Ophelia by Sir John Everett Millais, the tragic heroine lies dead, bedecked with flowers and clutching a posy of violets.

The violet is the symbol of Athens and, rather surprisingly, in Greece the flower is considered to be something of a sex symbol, much beloved by Aphrodite, goddess of love, and her son Priapus, whose predilections can be guessed at. It is also said that Persephone was picking violets and narcissi when she was abducted by Hades and taken down-down-down to the Underworld. In another myth, Orpheus was a gentle musician who played the lute so exquisitely that even the trees and mountains bowed their heads to listen. When his wife Eurydice died, Orpheus courageously descended to the Underworld to retrieve her, armed only with his lute. Hades was seduced by Orpheus' virtuosity and promised to return Eurydice, decreeing that she could leave, following her husband out of the Underworld, as long as Orpheus never once looked behind him on his long journey back to the world of the living. They were almost clear when he lost his nerve and glanced over his shoulder to see if Eurydice was indeed following him. In that instance all was lost; Eurydice was fated to return to the Underworld forever, and Orpheus, heartbroken, was left alone with only music to console him. The story goes that wherever he laid his lute, violets grew.

And so the violet is also the flower of faithfulness, mourning and melancholia. Children's graves in Greece were often planted with violets. Innocent, modest violets for the poor, lost babies.

Dog violets and *Viola odorata* are almost too small for pressing, for all but the most dextrous and patient of us, but if you persevere with care, they can make the most beautiful artworks, with their elegant, natural shape and flowers that jump up out of the leaves in a charming way.

PROJECTS FOR A PERSONAL TOUCH

The opportunities for creating artworks and decorative objects with pressed flowers are endless. Once you start to experiment, we have no doubt that you will come up with all sorts of ideas for how to create unique pieces with your pressings. The projects over the next few pages will give you some ideas to get you started using just a handful of basic materials. And remember, no two flowers are the same and nobody else will create what you create—embrace the idea that everything you make will be completely unique.

NAPKINS

Place a single pressed flower onto a freshly ironed linen napkin at each place setting. You can secure it using a ribbon tied around the napkin if dining outside, or tuck it into a fold in the napkin. Think about the season—violas, geum, and narcissi are perfect for a spring table; delphiniums, sweet peas, and cosmos for a summer dinner party; or hellebores in deep plum and white at Christmas. I did this for each guest at my own wedding instead of favours, which we felt were a bit unnecessary; mostly orange geums, chocolate cosmos, and yellow daisies tucked into each napkin. Throughout the day it was lovely to notice them popping up from suit pockets, tucked into friends' hair, and scattered around empty glasses on tables.

COASTERS

Pressed-flower coasters can be made at home by placing a single pressed flower into a silicone coaster mould and carefully pouring over clear epoxy resin, then leaving it to set overnight. Clear resin can be tricky to get right, the process involves meticulous preparation and accurate measuring. We recommend buying a crystal-clear epoxy resin kit, which will come complete with measuring cups, stirrers, and protective gloves. Crucially, kits come with clear instructions on how to mix the resin safely. When making our own coasters, we once mixed too much, not realizing epoxy resin is sensitive to both temperature and volume, at which point our colleague Scarlett came hurtling down the cobbled yard clutching a black plastic container at arms' length, smoke billowing out of the top and the sides beginning to melt with the heat. If too much of the resin and hardener are mixed together at the same time it can create an "epoxy exothermic reaction," where energy releases in the form of heat as the mixture catalyzes. Quite dangerous when caught off guard! Despite this mishap we have had successes; if you follow the instructions carefully and take care when preparing your materials, the results can be absolutely stunning.

If you don't fancy mixing your own resin, an easier way to make pressed-flower coasters is to place a single flower between two clear glass or acrylic discs—you can buy acrylic coasters online—fixing the two layers together using striped grosgrain ribbon stretched and glued around the edge.

Katie

GIFT WRAPPING

A little bit of extra effort when it comes to wrapping gifts always goes a long way. Paper can be plain—classic brown craft paper is a perfect blank canvas for any occasion and can be transformed into something glorious once you've had a rummage in your kitchen drawer for offcuts of ribbon or colourful string.

Layer silk and velvet ribbons around a plain gift box, tucking in long-stemmed pressed flowers in a complementary colour, or attach pressed flowers to plain wrapping paper with glue or tape to create your own unique gift wrap.

Glue individual pressed flowers onto paper gift tags leaving space at the bottom for a name; add a tiny strip of masking tape across the stem of the flower for extra security, if needed. This is a smart way of fixing tiny stems down if it feels too fiddly to use glue.

CHRISTMAS CRACKERS

Sometimes the best presents come in the smallest packages. We sourced these pre-cut craft-paper crackers online for our Christmas table. The design is fuss-free and offers a plain surface to decorate with pressed flowers and personalize with calligraphy.

When choosing your pressed flowers, hold each one between your thumb and forefingers and gently flex the stem to make sure it will bend without breaking. Some flowers will be more suited to a curved surface than others. Hellebores are the obvious choice as not only will they will be flowering at Christmas time, they also make excellent pressings, as do astrantia and butterfly ranunculus.

INSTRUCTIONS: First place the flower where you want it to go, marking the position lightly with pencil, if you like. Write the recipient's name now and let the ink dry before affixing the flower. Apply a thin layer of clear glue (we use Mod Podge) to the back of the flower head, the stem, and any leaves using a fine paintbrush, then carefully fix to the cracker. Leave for twenty-four hours for the glue to become touch dry.

Once glued, the stems can have a tendency to unstick when you bend the cracker into shape; if this happens, apply a touch more glue and a strip of masking tape across the bottom of the stem to hold it in place. Or simply decorate with just the flower heads and leaves. Tie a short length of velvet ribbon around the joins once you've filled the cracker to finish off your design.

Finn

LETTERS

One of the best marriages of two crafts is pressed flowers and calligraphy. Using a pressed flower to personalize a letter, to celebrate the birth of a child or mourn the loss of a loved one, is a lovely way to create a lasting memory. The next time you're passing an art supplier or stationery shop, pick up a few different papers and ink colours to experiment with. Often it's the tiny details that have the most lasting impact. Try simply fixing a single flower head to the back of an envelope once you have sealed it. This little gesture will go a long way.

INSTRUCTIONS: Always lay out your flowers first to decide where your text is best placed, then sketch in pencil before applying ink to paper. There is no right or wrong way, but embrace the natural shape of the flowers you're working with and play around with the spacing. Apply a thin layer of clear glue to the back of the flower head, the stem, and any leaves using a fine paintbrush, then position where you want it to go. Leave for twenty-four hours for the glue to become touch dry.

TIP: If you feel your handwriting isn't up to scratch, it might be worth investing in taking a calligraphy course—you will be amazed at the difference it can make.

GLASS BAUBLE DECORATIONS

We adore these elegant glass tealight holders, which can be adapted to make pretty decorations for all sorts of occasions. Decorate with hydrangea florets and hellebores to hang over your Christmas table or on your Christmas tree, or apply pressed "tête-à-tête" narcissi to the glass for an Easter decoration. Here we've used our favourite tiger-eye and bi-coloured violas and hung the baubles on willow branches with copper-wire fairy lights for a cosy winter arrangement. We've used battery tealights to avoid burning the flowers.

INSTRUCTIONS: Choose appropriately sized flower heads and apply a thin layer of clear glue to the face of the flower using a fine paintbrush, then carefully fix it on the inside of the bauble. You can apply another layer of glue over the back of the flower as a sealant if you like, but be careful not to go over the edges. You don't want to see glue smeared onto the glass. Leave for twenty-four hours for the glue to become touch dry before adding your tealights and using.

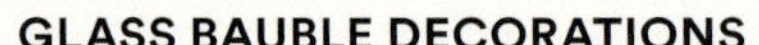

Story

FOXGLOVE

Deep, deep in wizardry
All the foxglove belfries stand.
Should they startle over the land,
None would know what bells they be.
Never any wind can ring them,
Nor the great black bees that swing them—
Every crimson bell, down-slanted,
Is so utterly enchanted.
"Foxgloves," Mary Webb (1881–1927)

All across the UK and Western Europe, extending into parts of Asia and North Africa, on heaths and in dappled woodlands, on rocky cliffs and in hedgerows, you will find magnificent stands of wild foxgloves, where they do their marvellous thing from spring to late summer. Often growing as tall as 2 metres (6½ feet) high, hanging their flowers on the sunny side of their downy, willowy stems, they are one of the most magical flowers; the subject of folklore, myths, and legends. Foxgloves are biennials (meaning they grow one year and flower in the second) that prefer acidic soil and in the right conditions produce so many seeds that if you just leave them be, there will always be a proliferation of new plants the following spring.

However bare the natural larder may be, animals will not touch foxglove seeds; they know instinctively that they will kill them. Foxgloves are, however, beloved by bees, their freckled tubular bells hum to the sound of the industrious little creatures burying themselves deep in search of nectar. One of the most charming myths about foxgloves is that, even when there is no wind at all, they appear to be bowing and curtsying, giving obeisance to the passing fairy folk. I suspect it is the busyness of the bees that creates this illusion, but late on a summer's evening, watching the foxgloves rustle and bob in the stillness of the forest in the gloaming, it is a story that is easy to believe.

The foxglove has been used for medicine, for working magic, for protection, and for communicating with faeries, elves, and woodland spirits. It has many names: lion's mouth, fairy caps, folk's glove, witches' thimbles, floppy-docks, and dead men's bells are just some of many. In France, it is known as "*gant de Notre-Dame*," or "our lady's glove." Although Wikipedia.fr remarks, "*La référence à Notre Dame est un invariant culturel des peuples Catholiques*" (the reference to our lady is a cultural invariant of the Catholic people), which made me laugh.

There are many theories surrounding the common name for *Digitalis purpurea*. The most likely seems to be that "fox" is a corruption of "folks," and

"glove" comes from the Anglo-Saxon word "gleow," meaning "a chime of bells." It's also true that the foxgloves' favoured habitats, in the dappled forests and shady glades, are a haunt of the cunning, secretive fox from whom they might get their name. In Norse legend, foxes wear a garland of foxglove corolla round their necks and the ringing of these fairy bells wards off the huntsmen and the hounds.

According to Ovid, the goddess Juno was furiously jealous when her husband Jupiter had a daughter without her. Minerva, the goddess of wisdom, medicine, handicrafts, and poetry, apparently sprang from Jupiter's head. To get even, Juno went to the goddess Flora and begged for her help in conceiving a child without the help of Jupiter. Flora slipped a foxglove bell onto her thumb, then touched Juno on the belly and the breast and Mars was instantly conceived. Juno departed for her confinement and had her child in Thrace, on the sea of Marmara. So Minerva was motherless and Mars was fatherless. Maybe this uneasy start in life accounted for Mars' bellicose behaviour. It must be difficult having a foxglove for a father.

Foxglove is extremely poisonous to humans and animals. If any part of the plant is ingested, it causes palpitations, delirium, hallucinations, vomiting, and, in extreme cases, death. But it is still used today as a vital heart medicine, to regulate the heartbeat and improve blood circulation. The difference between a beneficial dose and a lethal one is frighteningly small, so much so it would never be tolerated in modern medicine trials, but foxglove has been in use for over 200 years and is incredibly efficacious. Dr Withering, who discovered its usefulness for the treatment of heart disorders in 1785, did so by observing the effects of foxglove tea prepared by traditional herbalists.

It is suggested that Van Gogh took *Digoxin*, an extract of *Digitalis*, as a treatment for his epilepsy. Some art historians believe this to be the reason for the predominance of the colour yellow and the circular halos in many of his paintings. The ingestion of the plant can cause xanthopsia, which results in a yellow haze and distortion of vision in patients. We have a painting by Van Gogh of his physician, Dr Gachet, looking a bit sad and clutching a foxglove, but I'm not sure this is enough to prove this fascinating theory.

Foxgloves make gorgeous cut flowers. They last for ages and are spectacular in single-stem arrangements. In mixed bunches, according to various Victorian herbalists, they actually make the other flowers in the vase last longer. Foxglove tea was made out of the florets and added to the water of house flowers. At JamJar we love the ones with personality—those that have twisted and turned towards the sun. Their natural magical properties return our thoughts from the city to nature. One of our favourite flowers for the garden, and for cutting and pressing, is the lovely yellow Siberian variety, with its speckled corolla and graceful spires. In arrangements we like to combine the foxglove with its natural companions—spirea, briar rose, and cow parsley in the spring and grasses later in the summer.

We love to press foxgloves, especially the curly ones. Cut them when they are still small and before they have begun to set seed and you will get beautiful results.

Story

FERN

Here's a fantastic fact. Ferns have been living on planet Earth for more than 360 million years. They are 100 million years older than dinosaurs and 200 million years older than the first flowering plants. They are so successful as a species, they have hardly changed from their primeval beginnings. We know this because fern fossils have been found dating back to the Devonian period. They have not needed to adapt, they are not reliant on other creatures to pollinate them, they are entirely self-sufficient. Ferns were here long before us and will probably still be here long after we have gone. Perhaps they will be unfurling their beautiful fiddleheads for another 300 million years "when mankind has blown himself to bits, when England is not England. When not a soul is left to picnic on the blazing rocks" (Sir John Betjeman, "Beside the Seaside"). I hope so. Certainly they are a favourite of ours for the press.

There are as many as 10,650 known species of fern. They make their homes in many different environments, from moist and shady forests to cool mountainsides, arid deserts to bogs, swamps to dry crevices on rock faces. There are myriad shapes and forms; from the mighty tree fern to the delicate maidenhair fern, they are particular for their beautiful geometric shape and their way of uncurling new leaves, which start as a tightly bunched fist—known as a fiddlehead, because it looks exactly like one—and unravel into fully formed fronds. The word "fern" comes from the Dutch *Varen* or German *Farn*, meaning feather, referring to the classic fern shape and structure.

The Victorians were crazy about ferns; they even had a name for this obsession—"pteridomania"—which was coined by Charles Kingsley of *The Water-Babies* fame. (*Ptero* means feather or plume in Greek.) Ferns did very well in the poorly lit, over-crowded homes and gardens of rich Victorians. They also flourished in the grottos and rock gardens that were so fashionable at the time.

A book published in 1855 called *The Ferns of Great Britain and Ireland*, by botanist Thomas Moore, appeared at the height of pteridomania and featured marvellous illustrations by Henry Bradbury using nature printing—a method of printing that is most perfectly suited to ferns and seaweeds (but little else). In this particular method the plants were impressed into soft lead then electroplated to create printing plates from which exact replicas of the plants could be made. Bradbury patented the process after seeing the work of Austrian botanical illustrator Alois Auer, who had already published a book on nature printing in 1853.

Within quite a short time of pteridomania taking hold, botanists were already calling for native ferns to be protected from over-picking by zealous collectors who went to great lengths, even risking their lives, to gain specimens of rare species. A botanical guide called William Williams died while collecting alpine woodsia in Wales, his body was found at the foot of the cliff where Edward Lhwyd had found the species two centuries earlier.

But ferns were also something anyone could collect: a farmer, a miner or a botanically minded child could all have as fine a collection of foraged ferns as any young aristocrat on his "Grand Tour." This made these plants even more popular. There was even a magazine, first published in 1841, called *The Phitologist*, which catered especially to these fern obsessives.

In 1829, Nathaniel Bagshaw Ward invented the Wardian case, the forerunner to the terrarium, by accident when he noticed a fern that was flourishing in a sealed container in which he was keeping a moth cocoon. He had not opened the bottle for four years, yet still the fern thrived. He made his first cases to protect his precious fern collection from the heavily polluted London air, as he realized they created a perfect atmosphere in which ferns and other plants generated their own microclimate and maintained humidity. The Wardian case became a vital part of the botanist's and plant collector's repertoire. Plants could travel across continents with no ill-effects in a Wardian case, where previously they would, more often than not, have been killed by the salt spray or the inhospitable weather conditions of a sea voyage.

Tea, quinine and rubber plants all made their way to the UK and Kew Gardens in Wardian cases and Kew continued to use them for transporting plants right up until 1962.

Fashionable ladies liked to have a Wardian case in their homes, but there was always someone who had to go bigger and better. In 1850, Joseph Paxton, the architect of the magnificent Crystal Palace in London, home of the Great Exhibition of 1851, was commissioned to build a fernery at Tatton Park, in Cheshire, to house Charles Randall Egerton's fern collection. Tatton was not the only house to have a glazed fernery, but it is special because the handsome glasshouse still exists today and you can visit it. At one point they had to raise the roof to accommodate the giant tree ferns that luxuriated in the enclosed atmosphere.

Ferns were a popular motif in the Victorian era, with many of the great potters, ceramicists, and glassmakers using them for decoration. When the director of Kew, Sir William Jackson Hooker, died in 1865 at the age of eighty, a magnificent memorial was commissioned from Josiah Wedgewood and Sons in Jasperware. The plaque is a portrait of Hooker surrounded by beautiful ferns and can still be seen today in St Anne's Church, in Kew.

Just as they are becoming very popular for fabric and wallpaper design today, ferns were ubiquitous as the inspiration for Arts and Crafts design. I

remember, as a child, watching a beautiful Coalbrookdale cast-iron garden bench, with a pattern of ferns and blackberries, being hurled over a cliff on the Isle of Wight at the behest of its owner, to rust, decay and disappear into the sea. I remember being completely shocked as I watched this beautiful thing sinking into the sea; she had found a better bench, almost identical in design, but in plastic—"so much more convenient than that horrid heavy thing."

For many years botanists were confounded by ferns. They simply could not work out how they reproduced. Ferns are cryptograms and bear no fruit or flower, like mosses and lichens. The absence of seed was a puzzle for centuries and, because of this, ferns gained mythical status and many stories and legends were invented to explain the strange anomaly. The most famous of these tells of a magical fern flower that blooms once a year in the dead of night, on the eve of the summer solstice—the Feast of St John the Baptist. The seed was supposed to fall at the hour of his birth, accompanied by a great crash. However, it would not bloom if anybody was near, or if the flower was within hearing of the call of a rooster pronouncing the dawn. The bloom lasts just a single night and by morning it has disappeared.

The invisible seed of the fern became a well-known myth. If you could find a fern seed and carry it in your pocket, you too could achieve invisibility. Shakespeare refers to this in Act 2, Scene 1 of *Henry IV Part 1*: "We have

the receipt of a fern seed. We walk invisible." And in Ben Johnson's *The New Inn* (1629), a servant explains to his master why he was caught out: "I had no medicine to go invisible, no fern seed in my pocket." The invisible properties of the fern seed were so well rooted in folklore that the contemporary audiences would have known exactly what these passages signified.

Ferns, because of the mystery of their absent seed, were considered to have magical properties and were used as a protection against witches, spells, and evil spirits, and as an aid to vision and wealth. It is hard to imagine today how deeply entrenched the fear of witchcraft was in mediaeval culture, but easy to see how so much superstition grew around the mysterious fern, which flourished in dark and secret places. In the US, the smoke from burning ferns was used to exorcise evil spirits and ward off poisonous snakes. In Poland and Finland, the seed of the fern was believed to give access to the places where the supernatural creatures, or will-o'-the-wisps, guarded hidden treasure. Bracken, when cut on the slant, displays a distinctive sign that is variously described as looking like a devils hoof, an eagle, or the Greek letter X—a symbol of Christ. In Slavic mythology, ferns were plaited into girls' hair to protect them from the Rusalka—undead water sprites often thought to be of women who had drowned—who lurked beneath the surface of the lake ready to pull down unsuspecting swimmers. Of course, this is all great nonsense, but where there is no explanation, stories will arise to fill the vacuum.

Considered to have magical properties, ferns were used as protection against witches, spells, and evil spirits.

In 1539 Hieronymous Bosch, a serious and well-respected botanist and the author of *New Kreüterbuch* (1529), thought he had discovered the seed of the fern by staying out in the forest for four years in succession on the feast of St John the Baptist. On the fourth year of the experiment, he laid out sheets beneath the bracken and fell asleep. When he awoke at daybreak he found the sheets were covered in small dark specks and he believed his quest was over, but they were not seeds, as he thought, instead they were spores that had been released as he slept.

It was not until the mid-nineteenth century that botanists like the German Wilhelm Hofmeister and Polish Michal Hieronim Leszczyc-Suminski discovered the truth and exploded the myths with the (arguably more magical) explanation of how these plants actually reproduce, and how they have managed to do so for millenia. When conditions are perfect, the fern begins to germinate and releases its spores from the tiny little dots on the back of its feather-shaped fronds. From the spores, a completely different-looking plant about the size of a fingernail appears like a rootless, heart-shaped leaf. The new plant, called a prothallium, contains both male and female sex organs. Insemination occurs when conditions are damp and perfect. The male sperm has a tail that allows it to swim through water and fertilize the egg of a different plant, which, in time, grows into an embryo and a new baby fern is created. These are third-generation plants that are not remotely like their parents but do resemble their grandparents.

One method of making artwork with ferns is spore printing. When the fern spores are absolutely ripe they release millions of tiny spores into the atmosphere. If you catch a pregnant fern at the right moment and lay it on a piece of paper overnight, you can make a beautiful impression with the released spores. Uninterrupted, these spores will be puffed into the atmosphere, where they can travel for thousands of miles on the wind, or lodged in the fur of a passing animal, or the feathers of a bird.

Pressing ferns is an excellent place to start for someone new to the craft. They are generally quick to dry and their clean patterns make for very satisfactory pressings. They were not only used in nature printing, but also cyanotypes and spatter paintings, where you painted over the fern leaf and left its reverse pattern on the page. There is something deeply satisfying about the shape of the frond and its architectural pattern that has kept us fascinated for years.

Whole books have been written about ferns, and there are thousands of marvellous illustrations and botanical drawings, but few plants are as satisfactory to press as the mysterious fern.

FERN STAMP

Making a fern stamp using pressed flowers is an easy project for all ages, and a gentle way to encourage children to become more aware of nature. Sometimes it only takes a memory of a day well spent with an engrossed adult to trigger a lifelong fascination with botany. The beauty of using pressed ferns and flowers is they will lie very flat against the paper, making it easier to paint over them and create a solid silhouette, although fresh flowers can also be used to make nature rubbings, stencils, and ink stamps. To make our fern stamp we used watercolour ink and handmade 100 per cent cotton-rag paper, which has excellent strength and durability. We have recently discovered a 640gsm Khadi Paper, which is great here, as wet ink may make lighter papers curl. If you use a watercolour paper, choose those made with 100 per cent cotton—the paper will be acid-free and won't yellow with age, and colours will stay vibrant.

TOOLS

100 per cent cotton rag paper
Watercolour ink
Wide, flat paintbrush
Flowers used: lady fern (*Athyrium filix-femina*)

COMPOSITION

Lay the fern on the paper, angling the stem to make sure you leave some space around the plant to apply your ink.

APPLY COLOUR

Once you're happy with the placement and the fern is lying flat, apply ink to your brush, wipe off any excess, then brush outwards from the leaf spine. Take care as the dried leaves might be brittle. Even out the ink where there is pooling.

REMOVE FERN

Carefully peel away the fern to reveal the silhouette and leave the ink to dry.

Project

RAKESPROGRESS

Our flower-pressing story really started to get interesting when we designed an installation for a pop-up exhibition taking place on Floral Street, in the centre of London's Covent Garden (the street was aptly renamed in 1895 to reflect the trade of the flower market once situated nearby). The pop-up brought to life *Rakesprogress* magazine's stunning body of work, curated by the magazine's founders, Victoria Gaiger and Tom Loxley. *Rakesprogress* is a gorgeous magazine that takes a contemporary look at our ever-evolving relationship with the natural world; self-proclaimed as a celebration of the world of plants through the prism of art. We were one of several British florists invited to respond to the Covent Garden space—a huge, unoccupied, retail-shop-come-gallery with crisp white walls.

In the summer of the previous year, Victoria had written a feature on Jam-Jar Flowers for the fifth issue of her beautiful magazine. Thumbing through the pages of the issue as it landed on our doorstep, we were struck by a photograph of Christian Louboutin, the famous shoe designer, sitting casually on the edge of his bed with a wall of slightly faded pressed-flower specimens behind him. The quote beside the image read: "Louboutin's bedroom is bathed in early evening sunshine… Plastered into the walls are more than 100 panels of pressed flowers."

Made by a local doctor in the First World War, Louboutin had bought this collection of flower pressings at an auction around twenty years prior to Victoria and Tom's visit to his thirteenth-century chateau in the Vendée region of France. His bedroom was designed to house the collection, with the walls acting as the framework for each perfectly positioned, pressed-plant specimen. The walls had been designed to allow airflow through the cavity to prevent any moisture getting into the pressings.

It was this image in the magazine that not only inspired our designs for the exhibition but continues to influence our work. On an aesthetic level it was pure and beautiful, we couldn't help but admire Louboutin's devotion to his acquired collection. We love the idea that each and every specimen has a story, a place in history. It's hard to imagine the circumstances in which these plants were picked and pressed, the journeys they endured. And now they're part of another story, one in which they reside in this exquisite chateau, providing inspiration and a sense of calm, perhaps, to one of the most successful shoe designers of our time, who clearly has a deep admiration for the natural world.

For the exhibition, we designed a multi-panelled, pressed-flower artwork, consisting of fifty-two individual pressed flowers mounted on A3 boards, presented in a bespoke handmade frame. The artworks were float-mounted and left open without glass to invite the viewer in for closer inspection.

We had already started to build up an archive of pressings in the spring—including forget-me-nots, hellebores, and butterfly ranunculus—but this piece was made up mostly of summer flowers. Our specimens came from close by; most from Melissa's garden, some wild flowers picked from friends' land, and a few stems gathered on long walks in the countryside. We used

all the best wildflowers for pressing, such as carrot flower or Queen Anne's lace, wild scabious, poppies, vetch, and grasses, then added garden flowers such as butterfly ranunculus, California poppy, hellebore, and cosmos. This was the first time we had made individual artworks on A3 boards. We wanted to celebrate the simple forms of each individual flower, encouraging the natural curve of their windswept stems, and allowing them to each have their own space in the frame. Each specimen was labelled with its common and Latin names written directly onto the paper by our friend and talented calligrapher, Lu Guthrie.

So many friends and visitors to the exhibition spoke about a feeling of nostalgia on seeing the pressings, they seemed to strike a chord with everybody in some way or another, evoking memories of their childhood or transporting them to a bygone time. We were so pleased with the result.

The image of Louboutin's boudoir, an exquisite little jewel box of beauty, inspired us to push this idea a little further to create a piece of pressed-flower wallpaper, which we installed directly onto the gallery wall. First things first, it was important to find a beautiful paper. John Purcell Paper, a London-based, family-run business, stocks every kind of paper you can imagine in a treasure-trove of a warehouse not too far from our studio. Our choice was an off-white roll of heavy cartridge paper that had a subtle texture to the surface, which we had had cut to the width of a standard roll of wallpaper.

Without thinking about how we might take down our artwork after the exhibition, we slapped thick wallpaper paste onto a roll of lining paper and up it went, straight onto the wall, followed by our paper. Armed with an archive box full of our best specimens from the spring and summer season, we began laying out each one onto a long trestle table to work out a basic composition. We wanted the flowers to be compact, echoing a busy floral wallpaper print, so starting from the top and working our way down, one by one, we held up each flower until we found a positioning that felt right and balanced. Stems that had a natural curve were gently fitted in between straight stems and round flower heads.

Each flower was fixed into position with Mod Podge, our favourite acid-free craft glue. Once we had finished gluing all the flowers in place, we painted a thin layer of glue over the whole piece as a sealant to further secure and protect each pressed flower.

When it came to taking down the artwork, one of our guys, Ric, helped us, thinking it would be a nightmare getting it off the wall. As our backs were turned, we heard a crash as he whipped the whole thing off in one go and flopped it onto the gallery floor, in ten seconds flat. And it was perfect.

The exhibit is now proudly on show in our studio, framed and behind glass, and we use it as our control piece to observe how the different flowers change over time. It's been interesting to note the different rates at which they have faded—the ferns have bleached out completely, whereas the cosmos have retained almost all of the deep-pink colour in their petals. Creating this wallpaper was a project that really got us excited and made us realize there are endless possibilities we can explore with pressed flowers. It gave us a confidence to try all sorts of compositions that we hadn't attempted before.

SHOWN TO THE CHILDREN
LOWERS

Story

COSMOS

I must have flowers, always, and always.
Claude Monet (1840–1926)

The meaning of "cosmos" is the ordered universe. The opposite of chaos. It's a big name for a simple flower, but maybe simplicity is its key?

Cosmos are often cited in sacred geometry because of the orderly way the petals are arranged around a simple ovule. In its perfectly numbered petals, it is also used as an example of how the mathematical formula of the Fibonacci sequence occurs in nature.

Sacred geometry stems from a belief that there is a natural geometric plan in nature and throughout all the universe. In ancient monuments, churches, and temples from the Islamic world to Egypt and India, to our own cathedrals and parish churches, we find shapes and patterns recurring, often at a time when the cultures could not possibly be imitating each other. The inspiration for these wonderful shapes and designs must have been drawn from nature. Leonardo da Vinci's *Vitruvian Man* shows how the perfectly proportioned human form can fit into both a circle and a square. Unfortunately, not all of us are so perfectly formed. In the hexagonal cells of beehives, the spiral of the nautilus shell, and the simple structure of the cosmos flower, we can see how a perfect form occurs naturally and has inspired humans to make beautiful things for many centuries.

I always wanted to go to Mexico. I didn't get there until I was almost old, but it didn't disappoint. This is the country for flowers and colour; the food is colourful, even the celebrations of the dead are colourful! Flowers are everywhere—embroidered onto the dresses of girls, plaited into their hair, growing by the roadside and in pots, on balconies, in graveyards. Everywhere you go your eye is enchanted by colourful blooms. And of course Mexico is the native home of the cosmos, as well as of Frida Kahlo, who painted so many images of herself with elaborate floral headdresses, often with cosmos in her hair.

Imagine Hernán Cortés and the Spanish conquistadors arriving in this beautiful country, where they rode roughshod over historic civilizations, stealing their gold, tearing down their icons, dismissing ancient religions, and instilling a particularly cruel form of Christianity in their place. They brought with them their diseases and they took home whatever they could from the land: maize, avocados, tomatoes, papaya, beans and squashes, chilli peppers, and cacao. They also slipped the seed of the cosmos flower into their greedy pockets. Spanish priests back at home then cultivated the cosmos seeds in their monastery gardens and were so taken with this prolific, easily grown flower and its harmonious construction that they named it cosmos.

Chocolate Cosmos

In Spain, an eighteenth-century English ambassador's wife became fascinated with cosmos and collected thousands of seeds, then brought them back to the UK to plant. The flower quickly became popular and seeds were exchanged, bought and sold, and eventually taken back across the Atlantic to North America, where this flower became a favourite—especially in California, where it grows to this day. Not so far from its natural home in Mexico.

The cosmos is a forgiving flower. It is almost absurdly easy to grow and collect seeds from. It prefers poor soil, is reasonably drought-tolerant, and is a fantastic pollinator, attracting bees and butterflies, lacewings, and pest managers such as parasitic wasps and hoverflies. Like sweet peas, the more you cut the flowers, the more they reward you with blooms. Their bright, open-faced flowers continue from June until the first frosts, sometimes continuing to flower in my London garden until November. They manage well in pots and some species can grow up to 2 metres (6½ feet) tall. They make brilliant cut flowers and are excellent for pressing.

The more you cut cosmos flowers, the more they reward you with blooms.

At JamJar we love all the varieties of cosmos for flower arrangements and for pressing, but one of our favourites is *Cosmos atrosanguineus*. These elegant little flowers, native to Mexico, are known as "chocolate cosmos" not only for their velvety, maroon-brown petals but also for the way they smell distinctly of chocolate. Not, mind you, of the delicious rich aroma of Mexican cacao, more like a cheap Hershey bar, but definitely chocolatey, it can't be denied.

They also press wonderfully well. Their elegant foliage, long, slim stems, and their flat-faced flowers with little gold stamens make ideal subjects for the press.

New varieties of cosmos arrive every year. Check out growers like the brilliant Erin Benzakein at Floret Flowers, in Washington State, USA, who is constantly trialling new species in beautiful soft new colours; last year's favourite was "Apricot Lemonade." Sarah Raven, in East Sussex, England, developed the gorgeous "Double Click Cranberries," which is a firm favourite in my garden.

We love to grow and press the vibrant orange and yellow *Cosmos sulphureus* "Diablo," *Cosmos bipinnatus* "Sensation Picotee," with its distinct margins of dark pink, and "Cupcakes Blush," with pretty, frilled edges exactly like a paper baking case.

We can't recommend this flower strongly enough. Buy seeds of any coloured cosmos to grow blooms for pressing (colours are always better than white, which usually turn brown as they dry). They will give you enough stems to cut to use in the house as well as filling many presses and making your garden colourful all summer long.

Story

ANEMONE

There was once a road through the woods
Before they planted the trees.
It is underneath the coppice and heath
And the thin anemones.
"The way through the woods," Rudyard Kipling (1865–1936)

We love anemones at JamJar. We love the day, usually in mid-November, when the first Italian *Anemone coronaria* arrives in New Covent Garden Market. At the beginning of the season they are ruinously expensive, but very beautiful, and by Christmas they are a firm favourite, reasonably priced and long-lasting. Every year more varieties of this anemone appear with greater subtlety of colour, shape, and form. By March, the first English-grown anemones have arrived—*Anemone nemorosa* in the woods and *Anemone coronaria* in polytunnels and walled gardens—and there is a general feeling of "We are off!" Summer stretches before us with all its flowery magic ahead.

Anemones are close relations to the buttercup, and the family resemblance is most easily seen in *Anemone ranunculoides*, who have shiny little yellow flowers that appear in the spring, then die back to return again the following year.

In ancient woodlands, while the canopy is still bare, and as the sun gains a little warmth and the days begin to imperceptibly lengthen, a carpet of starry white flowers appears on the forest floor. *Anemone nemorosa*, or wood anemones, are an indicator of good forest management, because coppicing the canopy and leaving the ground undisturbed allows them to thrive. You will find these flowers where nature has only been interrupted with great care, where branches have been allowed to fall and rot back into the earth, and their rhizomes have been left undisturbed to creep by stealth underground. They are exceptionally delicate and beautiful, opening their faces into the sun and folding in their petals when the sky darkens. One charming piece of folklore asserts that when the petals are folded fairy folk sleep inside. *Anemone blanda* is the pretty garden version of *Anemone nemorosa*.

Anemones have inspired artists over the centuries. The flowers lend themselves in particular to the Impressionists, although there are wonderful examples of anemones by the Dutch Masters, too. A picture by Jacob Marel painted in 1634, when he was only twenty, is a particular favourite of mine. A still life with a tulip and anemones, a lily of the valley, and various bugs and butterflies, all depicted in such exquisite detail that you can almost see the caterpillar creep further up the stem of the tulip.

We love anemones massed in a vase with no accompaniment. There is something about them, as they continue to grow and unfurl, that makes your

fingers itch for a paintbrush. Henri Matisse was also inordinately fond of anemones. He painted them many times over, sometimes on their own, and often as the foreground in a picture with a languid woman in a loud shirt or a striped dress in the background. He obviously loved their unruly behaviour and enjoyed the way they twist and bend, with their long naked stems and the little pie frill of leaves. Van Gogh, Monet, and Renoir (who painted tomato-red anemones in his signature voluptuous style) were all fans. There are even more wonderful examples of anemones painted by Winifred Nicholson and William Nicholson, and Charles Rennie Mackintosh.

Anemones were a frequent motif of La Belle Epoque, and in particular Art Nouveau, which started in Paris at the end of the nineteenth century, and finished with the onset of the Great War in 1914. Rene Lalique, the renowned jeweller and later master glass artist, used anemones as a frequent motif in his exquisite work. In 1902 his contemporary and sometime rival, Emile Gallé, designed a bottle with painted anemones for the champagne brand Perrier-Jouët, which is still in use to this day.

Why did the Victorians, who set so much store by the language of flowers, assign the anemone with forsaken love and fragility? Is it because of the black heart of *Anemone coronaria* that the Persians and the Egyptians associate the flower with illness and the Chinese with death? We often use anemones when making winter funeral flowers; there is something about the fragility of the flowers with their dark hearts that suits a sombre arrangement, and tangles of pussy willow and early spirea with dark purple hellebores and white anemones seem to hit exactly the right note.

Anemones are beset with myth, the most famous being the tragic love affair of Venus and Adonis, wherein the gorgeous boy Adonis is gored to death by a wild boar. As the colour drains out of his face, the anemone flowers beside his dying body. William Shakespeare captured this moment in his epic poem "Venus and Adonis," in 1592–3:

> …the boy that by her side lay kill'd
> Was melted like a vapour from her sight,
> And in his blood that on the ground lay spill'd,
> A purple flower sprung up, chequer'd with white,
> Resembling well his pale cheeks and the blood
> Which in round drops upon their whiteness stood.

The Romans apparently picked anemones to guard against fever, and during the bubonic plague anemones were carried as protection. The first anemones of the spring were picked by young lovers in the Middle Ages and given as tokens, or sewn into the clothing of travellers, to keep them safe against pestilence and danger: "The first spring-blown anemone she in his doublet wove / To keep him safe from pestilence wherever he should rove" (Anon).

The Greek gods of the four winds, the Anemoi, sent these delicate little flowers ahead as a herald of spring and they are named for them. The anemone's most common familiar name is windflower, although it is unclear to which of the species wind lower actually relates. Apart from a nod to the Anemoi, the nickname windflower also indicates the anemone's fragility. Yet they must be tough little flowers to burst, as they do, to the surface, through the iron earth, as soon as spring is indicated. Other common names include thimbleweed and smell fox, which refers to their musky odour.

Just as *Anemone coronaria* and *Anemone nemerosa* are harbingers of spring, so *Anemone hupehensis* or *Anemone japonica* (Japanese anemone) is one of the last garden flowers of summer. The latter was named by Carl Thunberg, one of Carl Linnaeus' "apostles" or pupils, in 1784, who collected and pressed specimens while working as a doctor for the Dutch East India Company. The flower seeds were brought to Europe by plant explorer Robert Fortune after he discovered them growing around graves in a Shanghai cemetery.

The Japanese anemone is, in fact, not Japanese at all, but native to China, Taiwan, and Vietnam, although it has been naturalized in Japan for centuries. Like Thunberg before us, we find Japanese anemones are spectacular flowers to press, much easier and more satisfactory than *Anemone coronaria*. They are known in China as "broken bowl" flowers, with elegant, shiny, cup-shaped florets and bouncy little round seedheads held high above the leaf. Although they are far from home, they flourish in Western gardens and in their eager clump-forming proliferation they can even be considered as a menace or, worse, a weed.

Anemone pulsatilla or the Pasque (Easter) flower is another spring beauty that thrives in very poor soil; these flowers love the gravelly arid soil of a rock garden, or the chalky grasslands of Europe—although in the UK, their presence in the wild is much diminished due to loss of habitat. Just outside Cirencester, in Barnsley Warren, there is a Pasqueflower colony where over 20,000 plants flourish in the protected wildflower reserve. One of the most beautiful stages of pulsatilla is when it sets its ethereal and sculptural seedheads, from which the seeds can be whisked away and spread by the wind. Maybe the Pasqueflower is the original windflower.

An old folktale tells that these anemones are associated with pain and sorrow, and that you had to hold your breath as you passed a field of them so as not to become infected by the poisonous breath of the flowers.

Pulsatilla grows wild in the barren, overgrazed Sand County in Wisconsin, US, where the visionary ecologist and nature writer Aldo Leopold purchased 80 acres of ravaged land, previously destroyed by logging and forest fires. Leopold's book *A Sand County Almanac* is the story of his observation, love, and rehabilitation of the land. About the pulsatilla he said: "They endure snows, sleet, and bitter winds for the privilege of blooming alone." And "the chance to find one is a right as inalienable as free speech."

We prefer to press Japanese anemones and wild wood anemones, as the *Anemone coronaria* is slightly harder to handle, because of their thick legs and unruly frill, but with perseverance and frequent changes of paper throughout the pressing process, you can get stunning results, especially with the richer colours.

Project

DEVON

Our first pressed-flower commission for a private home was for a fantastic modern house on Dartmoor, in southwest England, for a couple who had seen the artwork we produced for the *Rakesprogress* exhibition at Floral Street. We were invited to pick and press flowers and ferns from the land surrounding their home to create a multi-panelled piece for a bedroom looking out over the landscape. We couldn't have asked for a nicer project, or client. David, the owner of the house, claimed to know very little about wild flowers, but it didn't seem that way to us. Within minutes of our arrival we were whisked off on a foraging adventure, with snips in hand and presses under our arms. It remains one of our favourite projects to date.

Dartmoor is a breathtakingly beautiful part of the world, even when it's blowing a gale and lashing with rain (which happens a lot). Craggy granite tors define the landscape, emerging from vast moorland, mostly covered by peat bogs fed by heavy rainfall. Combine all of that with very acidic soil and it could make for a pretty tricky environment for flowers to flourish in. However, the conditions mean the land has remained relatively undisturbed, and has never been intensively farmed; its diverse habitats have encouraged thousands of plant and flower species to find a home here, some unique to the area. Its rivers and waterfalls, blanket bogs, upland heaths, and ancient oak woodlands have created unique and varied ecosystems that have earned Dartmoor its Special Area of Conservation status. One of the most enchanting sites on Dartmoor is Wistman's Wood, a mysterious ancient woodland on the slopes of the West Dart River. Hundreds of species of lichen, mosses, and liverworts thrive there, covering every surface and dripping from the gnarled branches of stunted oak trees that grow in peculiar ways among moss-covered boulders on the forest floor.

Nestled in the heart of Dartmoor National Park, the setting for our pressing adventure was idyllic. The house was built into the hillside, its roof carpeted with wildflower turf, sheep nibbling from the sloping fields surrounding it. We spent a blissful couple of days collecting and pressing samples. Our brief was to press and preserve local woodland plants, moor and bog species common to the area, and we didn't have to venture far from the house to find a wide variety of specimens.

What was special about this commission, and perhaps why we look back on this project so fondly, was that it forced us to stop and really *look*. We spent hours combing tiny areas of the landscape searching for interesting species buried in the hedgerows, tucked into the crevices in the rocks, or on the banks of the pond at the bottom of the garden. The more we focused on a small area, the more we found; the more we looked, the more we saw. A mass of overgrown cow parsley at the side of the road suddenly becomes alive

with different wild species if you really take the time to observe. There was a feeling of calm about the whole process—there was nothing else to worry about. Our sole purpose over those two days was to search for flowers growing in their natural habitat, and to pick and press a selection of the ones that we found to be the most beautiful. Honestly, what could be nicer?

Up on the moors, bright yellow gorse bursts into flower in April, followed by swathes of pink and purple heather in the summer. But lower down in the valleys, where the soil is less acidic, is where some of the more delicate species thrive. We were overeager, arriving in late March for our first pressing trip to catch the early spring flowers, with a plan to return later in the season to search for more varieties. We found so many beautiful specimens that we never did return for that second trip. We searched for marsh marigold on the banks of the pond, as the bright-yellow flower favours damp spots, but sadly we were a week or two early. From the hedgerows we gathered recognizable species like wild Cambrian or Meconopsis poppies, red campion, herb roberts, and Queen Anne's lace. In the grass verges surrounding the house we found the cuckoo flower, otherwise known as lady's smock, which if seen in large numbers is a sign of damp ground. Its dainty stems and tiny lilac flowers—which open around the time the cuckoo starts to call—were perfect for pressing. In the meadows we picked red clover, buttercups, and

delicate grasses. We roamed the surrounding woodland in search of native ferns common to the area, with David as our guide and humble plant hunter. We picked modestly, especially in areas where there were only a few of the same species in flower. Our prized specimen was a particularly beautifully shaped wild strawberry that we found deep in a hedgerow.

Some specimens were pressed exactly where they were picked, while others were taken back to the house at the end of the day, where we worked at the kitchen table. Our samples were stored back at our studio in London, and were monitored carefully over several weeks, then organized into an archive as and when they were ready. We had labelled some of the lesser-known ferns at the time of pressing, but those without labels had to be identified with the help of our trusty wildflower guide—a much lengthier process than we'd hoped, as there are many minute discrepancies between species, but we got there in the end.

We always press more flowers than we need for the final artwork. This allows for failures in the pressing process, and also gives us flexibility when it comes to putting together the final compositions. Each specimen must stand alone as an aesthetically pleasing artwork, as well as working as part of the overall composition. We made around forty individual works, each labelled with their common and Latin names. To make the final selection of twenty-

eight panels and finalize the placement, our client joined us at the studio where we played around with layouts until we found a balance, taking into consideration the distribution of species as well as shape, form, and colour—a fun process that could have gone on and on.

The final selection is a mix of wild flowers and ferns—a celebration of each of these dainty specimens that grow within a few hundred metres from where they are now displayed. The piece was later framed in English oak by a local craftsman.

Species include: bluebell (*Endymion*), green spleenwort (*Asplenium viride*), lady's smock (*Cardamine pratensis*), oxeye daisy (*Leucanthemum vulgare*), wood speedwell (*Veronica montana*), daisy (*Erigeron karvinskianus*), red clover (*Trifolium pratense*), coral bells (*Heuchera*), marsh bedstraw (*Galium uliginosum*), wild poppy (*Papaver cambricum*), ragged robin (*Lychnis flos-cuculi*), maidenhair spleenwort (*Asplenium trichomanes*), wood vetch (*Vicia sylvatica*), cow parsley (*Anthriscus sylvestris*), red campion (*Silene dioica*), daisy (*Bellis perennis*), herb roberts (*Geranium robertianum*), cornflower (*Centaurea cyanus*), snake's head fritillary (*Fritillaria meleagris*), bulbous buttercup (*Ranunculus bulbosus*), deer fern (*Blechnum spicant*), wild strawberry (*Fragaria vesca*), milkmaid (*Cardamine pratensis*), broad buckfern (*Dryopteris dilatata*), black knapweed (*Centaurea nigra*), shining cranesbill (*Geranium lucidum*).

Three years on, David is very pleased with how the flowers are behaving, telling us: "Some have held the colour very well—the cornflower, buttercup and snake's head fritillary—but even where they have faded they still look very pretty. Some look positively ethereal."

Story

GERANIUM

First let's get the complicated bit out of the way. The cheerful window-box plant that many people think of and call a geranium is actually a pelargonium. Pelargoniums are about the most popular container and bedding plants in the world, they burst out in fabulous colourful explosions in hanging baskets, window boxes, and pots all over the Mediterranean. The ones that bloom most profusely are rarely scented. However, the more delicate the flowers are, the more delicious and fragrant are the leaves, sometimes smelling of rose, lemon, verbena, and mint. They are some of my favourite garden plants. In the UK, they do not winter well in the garden, usually being frightened to death by the first frosts. According to legend, geraniums (or maybe pelargoniums) first grew where the prophet Mohammed hung his coat to dry in the sun.

However, we are not talking about pelargoniums here but about hardy geraniums, also called cranesbill. The name comes from the appearance of the seedhead, which in many of the species forms into a long beak-like column that resembles a crane's bill. Eventually the seed pod ripens then splits open and the seeds are dispersed.

The humblest member of the cranesbill geranium family is *Geranium robertianum*, commonly known as herb roberts, with its tiny pink flowers and red stems, and also called red robin, death come quickly, stork's bill, fox geranium, and stinking bob. It is found throughout the UK and Ireland in woodlands and maritime shingle, on our city wastelands in scree, and in hedgerows in the countryside. It is also found in the northern Mediterranean from the Baltics to the Caucasus and right across North America.

It is believed that herb roberts was named after Robert of Molesme, an eleventh-century Cistercian monk who was evidently an extremely wise and pious man as well as a talented herbalist. The Cistercians were the farmer monks; their lives were ruled by the seasons and they rose with the sun and worked the fields. They were self-sufficient and spent much of their day working in silence or in prayer. Robert de Molesme became Abbot of Saint Michel-de-Tonnerre monastery and later was the founder of the Grande Chartreuse, the first Carthusian monastery. He was canonized by Pope Honorius III in 1222, a century after his death. I do hope the legend is true and that *Geranium robertianum* is called after this gentle man.

A favourite of the herbalists for centuries, herb roberts was used as a treatment for ailments of the liver and gallbladder, toothache, nosebleeds, and as a balm for wounds. When crushed, the leaves can be used as an insect repellent.

On the edge of the downs in the chalky dry soil we find masses of blue *Geranium pratense*, endless little saucer-shaped flowers all summer long, followed by masses of perfect cranesbill seedheads. They, like herb roberts and

Geranium sanguineum (otherwise known as bloody cranesbill), another wild geranium, make gorgeous pressings.

I also love *Geranium phaeum*, otherwise known as dusky cranesbill, the mourning or black widow. It is dark purplish-plum in colour, with long legs and tiny flowers that have backwards petals. When its seed beak forms and the seeds are ripe and I am working in my garden, I sometimes hear a little popping sound as the black widow spits her seeds far and wide. But she doesn't flower for very long and for those of us without much space we want the most we can get out of our garden plants.

There is a huge variety (about 300 species and many more cultivars) of these very forgiving perennial hardy geraniums that you can grow in your garden. They don't last long in the vase, but they flower profusely and being, on the whole, low-lying, they can cover up a host of sins and provide colour and interest at the front of the border. You can cut as many as you want for pressing and they will just come back at you with more flowers. They make beautiful pressings, too, especially if you can incorporate both flower, beaky seedhead, and bud in a single piece.

Story

POPPY

In Flanders fields, the poppies blow
Between the crosses, row on row,
That mark our place; and in the sky
The larks, still bravely singing, fly
Scarce heard amid the guns below.
"In Flanders Fields," John McCrae (1872–1918)

I first fell in love with the poppy in Dungeness, in Kent, on a perfect spring day in early July. Dungeness is the very edge of the world if you are English and were raised, as I was, in Sussex. It is a place of vast skies and low-lying country, with the grinding noise of lorries moving shingle from place to place in a vain attempt to stop the relentless encroachment of the sea.

We went to visit film director Derek Jarman's house and garden on the Dungeness shingle. Stopping the car, we crunched noisily across the stones to a modest shack with black clapboard walls and buttercup-yellow windows, and found we were in the most exquisite garden I had ever seen. Full of *objets trouvés*: fish bones, shells, old tyres filled with earth to make planters, coiled rope, tin pots filled with seaside flowers, and jumping out of that barren soil and salty shingle, pushing through the holes in rusty tins, were the poppies. Their delicate petals fluttered in the breeze that permanently sweeps across that barren place. In every colour, from cream through blush, pinks and oranges, and deep burnt sugar, the poppies bloomed. There were seed pods bursting with more seeds to assure another year of flowers. I slipped a couple into my pocket. I felt bad, but there were so many (and to keep a poppy blooming you have to remove the seedheads!). The few I pilfered still have their progeny in my garden in Brixton ten years later.

Papaver nudicaule, the Icelandic poppy, is the first to arrive in the flower markets. It is invariably a difficult flower. It has hairy legs and black feet due to having been quickly dunked in boiling water as soon as it is cut in order to try to preserve its short life span. This is how we find it, with its twisty, tortured stems. Often as many as half of your purchases won't come to flower, but oh, the reward when they do. Each bloom bursts out of the hairy pods that encase them, unfurling their rumpled, crumpled skirts until their golden hearts are revealed. This poppy comes in all shades—from a reddish-orange through yellow, salmon-pink, and white. Its meaty centre and propensity for the petals to fall apart make it a tricky flower to press, but when you get it right, it is marvellous.

Then there is *Papaver somniferum*, or the opium poppy, with its connotations of addiction and oblivion. It is the easiest thing to grow. Who could have known that these pale knicker-pink flowers with a black heart and

feathery centre much beloved by the bees could be holding the secret to the most addictive and deadly substance that grows on Earth? After a brief flower, the poppy sets seed. A fat, sculptural seedhead swells in the autumn sun.

I read a story a few years ago about a garden designer who bought a cottage and decided to create a garden out of the wilderness they had inherited. They began to clear the site, which had been left to run wild for many years, and as they dug, they turned up masses of old poison bottles. The garden was full of them. They came to the conclusion that the house must have once belonged to an apothecary. They continued to plan and plant a beautiful garden, but in early summer, as the garden began to bloom, masses of poppies appeared from nowhere. Some were very rare, like the Danish Flag Poppy—bright red with a white cross. They were bemused as they hadn't planted any poppies. But having disturbed the earth in the garden, the seeds that had laid dormant for almost a hundred years were triggered and bloomed in proliferation, as if woken from a deep sleep. The apothecary would have used *Papaver somniferum* to make painkillers and sedatives for their patients, and until the ground was turned over nobody knew what riches lay beneath the soil.

It is the fleeting nature of their appearance and the heartbreaking beauty of that short-lived flower that moves us.

We know from the World War I battlefields of Flanders, in Belgium, that poppy seeds can lie dormant in the ground for many years. But when the ground is disturbed, as it was by the soldiers who fought in that merciless conflict, the poppy seed will germinate and bloom. In Flanders, the irony of the blood spilt in that battle was echoed by an explosion of scarlet poppies the following spring. It is for this reason that to this day we wear a poppy on Remembrance Sunday, out of respect for our "Glorious Dead."

Then let us not forget the Reverend William Wilks, vicar of the parish of Shirley, in Surrey. The Shirley poppy was created in the 1880s after the reverend found a poppy in a corner of his garden adjoining arable fields—a variant of the field poppy that had a narrow white border around the petals. By careful selection and hybridization over many years, Wilks obtained a strain of poppies ranging in colour from white and pale lilac to pink and deep purple. And unlike the wild poppies, these had no dark blotches at the base of the petals. Further selection has given rise to semi-double and double forms, as well as flowers with a ring of contrasting colour around the edge, known as the picotee form.

As a florist, poppies are spectacularly difficult to use. Their delicate tissue-paper petals tend to fall apart as soon as they are picked. Yet it is the fleeting nature of their appearance and the heartbreaking beauty of that short-lived flower that moves us.

That said, poppies are the flower-pressers' dream. No flower retains as much of its shape and texture in the press as the poppy. No flower rewards the presser more. With this process, you can almost permanently preserve a cut flower that would normally last for only a few hours.

Project

LAMPSHADES

I have got two very pretty lamps that I bought a long time ago. They have etiolated brass stems with a circular base, a long, elegant brass switch, and braided-wire electric cables. They have had the wrong shades on them for years, and finding the right ones is something I had never got around to, but I knew what I wanted. I wanted a parchment-paper shade and the shape had to be just so—narrow at the top and wide at the base. I finally found them by chance, and while we were installing them I thought, this could be a fine vehicle for pressed flowers. So I took them to the studio where our colleagues Storm and Sally were working away making up artworks.

We had a discussion about the inevitability of how a lampshade decorated with pressed flowers, with its constant exposure to light and possibly heat, would not be a good place for colourful flowers. We agreed that whatever flower we used should be an exquisite shape so that they would still be beautiful even if they lost colour. I left them on the table and went to do something else. When I got back Storm was deep into the archive drawers. She knew what she was looking for, and with a little shout of glee she alighted on some dicentra, which have pretty, arching stems of heart-shaped flowers through which, if you shine a light, you can see the seedheads forming. They had lovely leaves and the stems were not too brittle, so we knew they would stick well to the curved surface of the lampshade. We all agreed these were perfect for our project.

The lampshades are actually tiny, so a couple of flower stems and a pretty leaf or two was enough to decorate both. We laid these out on the shades and fixed them in place using tiny strips of masking tape. As a pair I wanted them to be friends but not identical, and to not look as if they were printed.

Once the design was in place, we started the gluing and sticking process, just as we do for all our projects with paper. India came back to the studio and loved the design, and began to fix the flowers into position. I took them home to try them on the elegant lamp stands. They looked stunning.

I am looking forward to seeing how they cope with time. Will the wear and tear of everyday life, the banging on and off of lights twice a day (we don't have a very sophisticated lighting system in my house) mean they only last a few weeks or months, or will they endure for years? Will our grandchildren be fighting over who keeps them for their children? It doesn't very much matter, this was not an expensive or very time-consuming project to complete, and for now, it just looks so beautiful.

TIP: Choose flowers that are still flexible when pressed—brittle stems are no good for curved surfaces. Other suggestions for suitable flowers include astrantia, pansies, field poppies, wildflowers, and *Ammi majus*.

Story

WEED OR FLOWER

A weed is but an unloved flower!
Go dig, and prune, and guide, and wait,
Until it learns its high estate,
And glorifies some bower.
A weed is but an unloved flower!
"The Weed," Ella Wheeler Wilcox (1850–1919)

"A weed is a flower growing in the wrong place." This idea was first expounded by George Washington Carver (1864–1943). Carver was a remarkable man, born into slavery but raised and educated by a white family, who went on to become the most important black scientist of the twentieth century. He recognized that the soil of the cotton fields was being severely depleted by the constant repetition of a single crop, so he encouraged poor farmers to rotate their cotton crops with peanuts, soya beans, and sweet potatoes, thus improving the efficiency of the land. He was a great man and he loved flowers, and weeds too, presumably. He was also a fine botanical artist. There are dried specimens of plants that he collected on display in the museum that bears his name in Tuskegee, Alabama, where he taught for forty-seven years.

The term "weed" was coined in the eighteenth century by Jethro Tull in his nicely alliterative book, *Horse-hoeing Husbandry*. But what makes a flower a weed and why are they reviled by gardeners everywhere? I think it is mostly because they are the thugs of the garden. They reproduce fast and take over quickly, often strangling, threatening, and killing other more precious and less-robust plants. One of the weed's most powerful tools is seed dormancy. Weeds can leave viable seeds for many years in the ground, awaiting optimum conditions for them to grow. Lotus seeds collected from the bottom of a Manchurian lakebed in China were discovered to still be viable after 1,000 years of lying dormant.

But if we wipe out all the weeds we may do ourselves a great disservice. In the wild, weeds are often important nitrogen-fixers, pollinators, and soil regulators. Plants that are considered weeds by some are actually vital to the natural balance.

In the city, *Buddleia davidii* is one of the most prevalent weeds. It can take hold on railway lines and in tiny cracks in brickwork. It is not uncommon to find a derelict house with buddleia growing out of the roof and the chimney stacks, threatening the whole stability of the structure. It is extremely difficult to get rid of it once it has taken hold, but there is no plant so beloved by butterflies. Call it the butterfly bush and catch a whiff of its honeyed scent on a summer's evening when the flowers are heavy with feeding butterflies, and suddenly it doesn't seem like such a bad thing.

Poppies are weeds when they grow among corn plants, but they are also one of the most important flowers when grown as a crop to produce morphine—the most efficacious painkiller known to medicine and a drug that has eased many tormented souls as they wrestle with disease and excruciating pain.

In my own garden, bindweed has been a recurring problem. When we moved in, the next-door garden was full of bindweed. It grew so fast I could map its progress as it scrambled along a wall and up a willow tree three gardens along. It crept under my fence and twisted its way up the clematis and roses I had planted, strangling the new shoots and flowering merrily out of my reach. I started to slowly dig it out. It became an obsession; tracing the long, white, naked roots with my bare hands, making sure to get the whole lot up in one go, because if you snap the roots or leave the smallest piece in the earth, it will regenerate and start again. A nice gardener I consulted just advised me to keep pulling it out and eventually it would get bored and head off in another direction. And that is what apparently happened, although the roots still sneak back occasionally if we do not keep a constant watchful eye out.

Dandelions are another weed, and these have terrifyingly strong taproots that bury themselves deep into the soil. Especially favouring cracks in brickwork and concrete, they are hard to uproot and their efficient seedheads mean they proliferate at a tremendous rate if they are allowed to. And yet what flower has a sunnier face or a more ravishing and evanescent seedhead? Dandelion gets its name from the French *dent de lion*, or lion's tooth, which refers to the tooth-like indentations on the leaf. Both flower and leaf are edible; in fact, a salad of young dandelion leaves is delicious, and when we were children, we were encouraged to pick them to feed to our guinea pigs, who appeared to enjoy them hugely too. Its common names include the English "pee-a-bed" or "wet-a-bed," or the French "*pissenlit,*" referring to its strong diuretic qualities. Dandelions are experts in survival, and unless you get the whole root out they will just return healthier and stronger than before. They have become so resistant to a lot of the chemicals designed to get rid of weeds that often they are the last men standing. Fields of gold stretch out where nothing else will grow, where all other vegetation has been obliterated. Still the dandelion stands unvanquished, setting its seedheads to be blown away in the summer breeze. Luckily, they are beloved by bees and other pollinators, because the farmers certainly don't feel the same way about them.

Weeds are not always unlovely, a hedgerow filled with bindweed, groundsel, ragwort, poppies, corncockle, and loosestrife all buzzing with bees and bugs and butterflies is a beautiful sight. Just not in my backyard, thank you very much.

Weeds are viewed as unruly bullies, dangerous, amoral, and promiscuous. They challenge our sense of order and make us feel unsafe, invaded, and out of control. John Ruskin, the ultimate nineteenth-century prude, viewed them as degenerates. His contemporary, Charles Darwin, on the other hand, observing his weed patch at Down House, saw that the hardiest species would eventually take over and thus developed his theory of "survival of the fittest," or natural selection. Therefore it is rather strange that we use the word "weed" in reference to a human being to describe someone weak and feeble—the very opposite of a thug. Although, many so-called weeds disguise their thuggishness behind a delicate and fragile appearance.

If you google "weed" your screen will be flooded with masses of images of the marijuana plant. The weed reference appears to have first come into the American vernacular around 1929 during Prohibition, when alcohol was banned and people smoked weed to alter their moods. "The humble 'reefer,' 'the weed,' marijuana, or [whatever you call] a doped cigarette, has moved to Park Ave. from Harlem," wrote the *Chicago Defender* in 1932 about the change in the people who were using cannabis. If, however, you add an "s" to your google search, you will get quite different results.

Plants that are considered weeds by some are actually vital to the natural balance.

Nettles—*Urtica dioica*—for instance, were the bane of our lives for us children running through the fields with bare legs. We were frequent victims of these stinging nettles and despite the frenzied hunt for dock leaves to ease the pain, the rash could last for several hours. But nettles are marvellous for wildlife, and in particular butterflies, as they are the primary food source for the caterpillars of tortoiseshell, peacock, and comma species. They are also favourites of aphids, who in turn make themselves useful as tasty snacks for birds, and they are a beloved habitat of ladybirds, who eat the aphids and are generally the gardener's best friend. Nettles are also very useful in a compost heap, and when boiled up in water they make an excellent (if very smelly), nitrogen-rich plant food. They are edible and a great source of iron, calcium, and magnesium—nettle soup is delicious and nettle tea is said to have many benefits for asthma, eczema, and hay fever sufferers. Infuse young leaves in boiling water, add honey and a slice of lemon. You can also make a good, strong rope or "cordage" from the stems of nettles. So the nettle, is it friend or foe? A weed, or a superfood?

Green alkanet, with its bright blue flowers, is often mistaken for borage or comfrey, and it is a thug I could do without. Unlike the nettle, it seems to have few virtues; its roots are used for making a red dye and it is attractive to pollinators. It's not a completely unattractive flower, but there are so many more beautiful blue flowers, like forget-me-nots or its aforementioned cousin borage, which are just as bug-friendly and much easier to control.

Are brambles a weed? Or are they the providers of delicious free blackberries? Certainly trying to get them out of the garden when they have taken hold is painful work, but they can't be too bad because both flower and fruit are so delightful. It's another thorny question.

In the Garden Museum beside Lambeth Bridge in London, there is a wonderful scrapbook of pressed flowers assembled by Jane Lindsay, who gathered them from bomb sites in the City of London. During World War II, much of the city was bombed, and for a long time afterwards, the sites were left untouched as London crawled out of the financial and physical wreckage caused by the conflict. The botanist Edward Lousley noticed an explosion of spontaneous flora appearing in the rubble; before the war he estimated that no more than twenty wildflower species were growing in London, but by 1944 over 100 species had been observed and identified by naturalists and keen amateurs. Much hope was derived from this proliferation of new life emerging out of the devastation. An article in *The Times* written by the botanist E. J. Salisbury noted that: "Wildflowers had spread over the bomb sites: rosebay, willow herb, coltsfoot, groundsel, Oxford ragwort, Canadian fleabane, thornapple, and thanet cress."

Perhaps the most pernicious weed of all, though, is Japanese knotweed—*Fallopia japonica*. Native to East Asia, it is incredibly fast-growing, with strong, bamboo-like stalks that form in clumps and can reach up to 2 metres (6½ feet) high. A not unattractive creamy white flower forms in late summer. It is classified as a pest and is a phenomenally invasive species. In the UK it is an offence to grow knotweed and if you are caught fly tipping it, or leaving it in your green waste, you can be prosecuted. The weed is so hard to eradicate that if you buy a property where it grows, you may not be able to get a mortgage until you can prove that the land has been clear of it for three years. Yet even Japanese knotweed is not without its uses. In Japan, the flower is valued as a source of delicious "bamboo honey," and the tender young stems are eaten as a foraged vegetable. It is used in traditional Chinese and Japanese medicine, and ground-feeding songbirds eat the seeds.

If we think we have problems with weeds in Europe, we need only look to the forested areas of West Bengal, which have become infested with *Mikania micrantha*, otherwise known as "the mile a minute" weed. It can grow up to 90 millimetres (3½ inches) in twenty-four hours and reaches up to 6 metres (20 feet) tall, smothering everything in its path. A single stem can produce as many as 40,000 seeds, which are dispersed by the wind. Now, that's a weed.

Weeds are having a good moment just now, as they did during the Arts and Crafts movement of the late nineteenth century when the celebration of *Rus in Urbe* (nature in the city) was fashionable, and artists like William Morris and Charles Voysey incorporated daisies and dandelions into their textile designs. Similarly, today people have understood that a weed need not necessarily be a bad thing. Perfect green swards in our parks are being replaced by wildflower meadows; where most of those flowers would once have been considered weeds, and still are, in many places. Fortunately for us, these make lovely pressings.

GROWING FOR PRESSING

The great thing about growing flowers to press is that you don't need masses of space or years of gardening experience to get started. You can make beautiful pressings from just a handful of cuttings, so whether you have a generous garden or a tiny space with room for just a few pots, as long as you choose your flower types wisely and plan ahead, you can grow flowers to press from spring right through to autumn.

The most productive way to grow flowers for pressing is to concentrate on easy-to-grow annuals, especially if you don't have a lot of space. Cut-and-come-again varieties are the best value, as they will keep producing more and more flowers as you keep cutting. Cosmos, sweet peas, and Californian poppies are perfect examples, and some of our favourites to press. They produce masses of blooms if they are well cared for and will flower right through the summer until they set seed, or up until the first frost.

We grow as many flowers for pressing as we can in Melissa's garden; some seeds sown directly into the earth, but most into containers. Many of the pressed flowers that we've used on our most ambitious projects were grown here and pressed on the kitchen table. We are slowly but surely transforming this modest space into a productive cutting garden. Annuals can be bought as young plants from your local garden centre, but growing from seed is easier than you might think and so much more rewarding. Last year was the first year I had ever attempted to grow flowers from seed at home. I'm a beginner when it comes to gardening and have a tiny outside space, but as soon as my little seedlings started to sprout it felt miraculous and I was completely hooked.

GROWING FROM SEED

If, like many of us, you don't have the luxury of a potting shed or greenhouse, the kitchen table and a cool windowsill will do just fine to get seeds started. If you think you'll be growing more and more from seed you might want to invest in a propagator, which acts as an incubator with controlled conditions and helps kick-start germination. Some annuals, like poppies, prefer to be sown directly into the garden or a container where they will grow, as they don't like their roots to be disturbed, but most can be grown in seed trays to be potted on. Sowing seeds in the spring will give you flowers from early summer through to autumn, and sowing hardier varieties in autumn will flower the following spring. Don't forget to label your seed trays with the flower species so you can keep track of your seedlings. Once your seeds have germinated and their shoots have grown a couple of inches, you need to move the seedlings outside within a few weeks to acclimatize before planting out. They won't quite be strong enough to face the elements, so it's worth protecting them in a cold frame—a simple structure built low to the ground with a transparent roof to let light in—until the weather becomes consistently warm and the threat of frost has passed.

SWEET PEA

Flowering: May–September

Sweet peas are the first seeds to sow, as they're tough, able to withstand frosts, and germinate easily without the need for heat. Everyone has their own way of growing sweet peas, but we'd recommend starting to sow seeds as early as December. These flowers are easy to grow and will produce gorgeous scented blooms all summer, as long as you keep cutting. Towards the end of the season, cut and press their long stems and curly tendrils to capture their lovely shape and structure. If you're buying young plants from the garden centre, often one small pot will have several plants in it that can be separated out into a larger pot. Be careful not to overcrowd your planter. One of our favourite varieties for pressing is sweet pea "Cupani." This fragrant sweet pea is one of the oldest varieties that can be grown as an annual, and if left in a warm, sheltered spot it will return year after year.

Sow single seeds in winter into a root trainer or cardboard loo rolls filled with potting compost. Sweet peas form long roots that need space to branch out, so this extra depth is essential to develop a healthy and happy plant. Mice love sweet peas, so make sure your seeds are covered or protected from these hungry pests. When your seedlings appear, keep them cool to encourage root growth rather than stem growth, as this will ultimately lead to a stronger plant and lots more flowers. Store in a cool spot indoors, a garden shed, or cold frame with plenty of light.

Pinching out the tips will encourage side shoots to form, resulting in a bushier and healthier plant—this is a must if you want lots of flowers for pressing. When your seedlings have four pairs of leaves, simply pinch off the growing tip with your thumb and forefinger.

It is important to create a support system before planting out your seedlings. Use bamboo cane or birch twigs to create a teepee and stake it securely into the soil. Plant out your seedlings when the weather is warm enough. Containers must be deep with drainage holes. Fill with rich soil—sweet peas are greedy, so add manure to the mix to help retain water. Plant your seedlings at least 10cm (4 inches) apart. As they begin to grow, thread their stems through the support frame and tie them into position with twine or string, as this will strengthen the plant as it grows. Sweet peas will always be angling to produce seed quickly, so keep your eyes peeled and snip off any seed pods as soon as you see them forming. If you let the seed pods take over, that's the end of the flowers. As the first flowers appear, start cutting straight away. The plant will thrive on being cut.

COSMOS

Flowering: June–November

A fantastic container plant, cosmos are a must-grow for pressing. The more you cut, the bushier the plant will get and the more flowers will grow. "Antiquity" is one of our favourite varieties; it is great for small spaces, as it has a shorter stem than most, so it works really well in smaller containers. Melissa always has cosmos in all different tones of pinks dancing high in big stone troughs in the garden, flowering all the way through the summer, often as late as October or November. Sow in early spring, and a few more in late spring to give you flowers all the way through to autumn.

Plant seeds into modules or seed trays two at a time—there are now lots of great biodegradable growing trays available, made from wood fibre rather than plastic. Cosmos need heat to germinate, around 20°C (68°F) is ideal, so place your seed tray on a heat mat or a sunny windowsill in March and April, and rotate regularly so they don't grow in one direction towards the light. If both seeds germinate, remove one by gently lifting with your fingers from the soil and leave the stronger one to grow, then move the tray away from the heat. As your seedlings grow, keep potting them on into bigger pots, adding more potting compost each time to help their root system develop.

Plant out when all danger of frost has passed; cosmos are half-hardy, so they do not cope well with very cold temperatures. Try to avoid soil that is too rich, as this can cause the plants to become tall and leggy. Keep cutting! Just like sweet peas, the more you cut, the more flowers will grow. Follow the stem down to where it meets the leaf and cut just above the leaf to encourage a new bud to form.

CALIFORNIAN POPPY

Flowering: June–September

If we had more space, we would love to grow poppies in all sorts of varieties, they are my absolute favourite and a dream to press. But with limited growing space we have to choose wisely. Californian poppies are a brilliant variety for pressing. They are easy and quick to grow from seed, forming low with pretty foliage that froths out when planted in a container. Other varieties like opium or oriental poppies, with their tall, straight stems and heavy heads, are better grown in the garden where they can be staked for support if needed.

Poppies do not like to be moved, so sow seeds directly into the ground or into the container where you want them to grow in spring. They like poor, well-drained soil, so add lots of grit or gravel, then sow thinly, around 10cm (4 inches) apart, otherwise you will spend hours thinning them out later. They need light to germinate, so sow seeds on top of your soil and place in a sunny spot. Carefully thin out seedlings when they are around 10cm (4 inches) tall to leave around the same distance, 10cm (4 inches), between each one, if needed. Water regularly to prevent poppies from drying out, but don't leave them sitting in waterlogged soil or their roots could rot. Keep cutting and removing seed pods, and more flowers will come.

NIGELLA & CORNFLOWER

Flowering: July–September

Nigella and cornflowers are both hardy annuals, so they can be sown directly into the garden or a container in spring. If you have space, you can extend their flowering season by sowing some seeds in autumn, which will then start to flower as early as mid-May. Both plants should survive over winter without the need for extra protection from the cold.

I'd say they're not quite as good value as sweet peas or cosmos for container planting, as you need a lot of them to make an impact. They also grow tall and leggy, so they can need extra support. But if you have more space, they are easy to grow and are both cut-and-come-again favourites of ours for pressing. Make sure you leave some flowers to form seed pods towards the end of the season, as they will self-sow to give you another crop for free the next year.

AUTUMN BULBS

The leaves on the trees have begun to turn, there's a chill in the air, you still have a few flowers blooming, but the seed pods are forming and your presses are full. Now is the time to think about buying bulbs to plant indoors in pots over winter. For early spring pressings choose tiny *Narcissus* "Tête-à-tête" and crocus, snowdrops, and snake's head fritillaries, as well as tiny tulip varieties like clusiana, "Lilac Wonder," and *T. turkestanica*, and lots of colourful primulas. Bulbs are cheap to buy, and although once the flowers have been cut they won't come back in the same season, the bulbs can be kept in the pots or dried and stored to plant the following year. Plant them in low bowls, ceramic pots, or anything you like. Taller narcissus varieties might need staking with birch twigs for support. If you're clever, you can layer a variety of bulbs in deeper pots to provide a succession of flowers throughout the spring months. The master of container planting, Arthur Parkinson (@ arthurparkinson_), author of *The Flower Yard*, can teach you how to plant a magnificent "bulb lasagne."

WINTER-FLOWERING PLANTS

Once your annuals have set seed in the autumn, you can replace container plants with winter-flowering plants, which you can buy from your local garden centre or flower market. These varieties are not cut-and-come-again, so make sure you get plenty of enjoyment from them before you snip them.

HELLEBORE

We always find it hard to resist hellebores when they arrive in the flower market in the depths of winter, just as we're fed up with dried flowers and desperate to see some new life. A winter-flowering perennial, hellebores can be enjoyed indoors over Christmas before being planted out into a container or straight into the garden where they will thrive, flowering right through to the end of spring. Once cut, their flowers will take a long time to come back, so they are more of an investment as a plant for pressing. If you have room to plant hellebores into the garden, they will self-seed and come back year after year. To enable the plant to continue in the garden the following year, you will have to resist the urge to cut for pressing and wait for the first seedheads to form.

We love to press *Helleborus orientalis*, as they have a slender stem and pretty markings on their petals. "Pretty Ellen Spotted" and *Helleborus orientalis* subsp. *abchasicus* (this one is early flowering, often in time for Christmas) from Sarah Raven's nursery are both gorgeous.

VIOLA

Perfect for tiny spaces, violas are excellent value for money and will bring lots of lovely colour to your outside space with relatively little maintenance. We tend to buy plants rather than trying to grow from seed because they are more challenging to germinate, and because plants are such great value for money. Buy plants in January for a burst of colour through the cold and dark months. Although they are rela-

tively easy to look after, they have delicate roots, so go easy on the watering. Cut flowers when they are looking their best for pressing, and more will come, and pinch off any dead heads. If you can bear it, try tapping off the soil and rinsing the roots to press the whole plant, it is a time-consuming process but so worth it. Viola "Tiger Eyes" is a new favourite of ours. The backs of their petals are deep purple, appearing unassuming at first, but open to reveal a deep-yellow ochre and burnt-orange face with dark brown tiger stripes.

SELECTING YOUR SEEDS

Milli Proust and Sarah Raven are two of our go-to growers for annual seeds. Milli is a grower with exquisite taste who is championing small-scale growing from a little patch in West Sussex. Her seed packets are printed with her own botanical illustrations on recycled paper, which quite rightly send her Instagram followers into a frenzy of excitement. We admire her choice of varieties and gentle colour palettes; some of our favourites for pressing are: cosmos "Apricot Lemonade," *Ammi majus* "Graceland," larkspur "Misty Lavender," poppy "Amazing Grey," and *Nigella* "Persian Jewells."

Sarah Raven sells a huge variety of annual seeds online, many of which are exclusive to her, so it's always fun to browse her vast collection. Her newsletters and website are a fantastic resource for gardening advice and inspiration. If you are short on space, or not so keen on growing from seed, you can buy seedlings in single or mixed varieties, which is super helpful if you want to press flowers that are more difficult to grow from seed, such as phlox or violas. Another tip is to buy Arthur Parkinson's book *The Flower Yard*. Arthur grows almost all his plants in containers in a tiny space outside his front door—his flower choices, colour schemes, and planting methods will inspire anyone with a slight inkling to grow their own. As well as being a really useful and practical guide, it is full of the author's charm and humour.

Order your seeds as early as you can in the autumn to get what you want before they sell out. And, as in my case, try not to get too excited and order too many —you don't want to end up with endless trays of seedlings with nowhere to plant them. Often, less is more. Think about what you want to create with your pressings as well as how colours and shapes will work together in your space.

Story

IRIS

What in your life is calling you,
When all the noise is silenced,
The meetings adjourned…
The lists laid aside,
And the wild iris blooms
by itself
in the dark forest…
What still pulls on your soul?
Rumi (thirteenth century)

Very near the JamJar studio there is an iris garden. It is on the corner of a modest street that we often drive past in the Jam Van. For most of the year it is unexceptional; then suddenly in May it blooms. Masses of pale blue irises, every year more and more, and now the owner of the ground-floor flat has introduced more species and there are brown and yellow irises too. From year to year we forget all about it, then we see it again and have to slow down and stop the van to step out to gaze on them. Van Gogh's astonishing paintings of irises come to mind.

Van Gogh voluntarily committed himself to the asylum in Saint-Paul de Mausole in Saint-Rémy after several incidences of what would now be considered hypomania or bipolar disorder. He had also been a victim of self-abuse, having recently cut off his own ear. It must have been something of a relief to enter the relative calm of the asylum and set up his easel in the garden to paint the irises growing there. In the tortuous twists and turns that the irises take, we see some little way into Van Gogh's troubled mind. He described his work as "the lightning conductor for his illness;" he felt that painting grounded him, made him feel sane again. Yet there is beauty, too. *Irises* is a remarkable observation of the nature of flowers. The painting is full of light and air, even joy; one single white iris has caused much speculation as to its meaning by art experts. I personally think he painted what he saw, a mass of blue irises with a single rogue albino among them. For several years one of Van Gogh's iris paintings held the record for being the world's most expensive painting. It sold in 1987 for $53.9 million—a bitter irony for the artist who sold only one or two paintings in his entire short life.

Van Gogh's description of his painting has a striking resonance with the goddess Iris in Greek mythology. Iris was the one who connected heaven to earth, often appearing as a rainbow. She was married to Zephyrus, god of the west wind. She was the messenger between the gods and humans, fleet of foot and swift on the wing, she travelled at the speed of light. There was no limit to where she could go. She could travel from the highest heavens

to the bowels of the Underworld, hurtling through cerulean skies into the depths of the wine-dark sea. She watered the clouds and created rainbows, which she used for transportation. A heavenly courier bringing messages from one god to another. I can't help feeling her marriage with Zephyrus might have been a bit hectic, with them both huffing and puffing and whirling and whizzing about the place. Iris is often portrayed with a vase or ewer in which she carried nectar to the gods; she also used this vessel to collect water from the River Styx in the Underworld. When the gods had to swear an oath they also had to drink the water from Iris' ewer; if they were not truthful, straightaway they would be rendered unconscious for a year. The goddess Iris, with her vase and her beautiful iridescent wings, is the inspiration for the beautiful flower that took her name.

The genus *Iris* contains around 300 species; they are perennial, growing up from creeping rhizomes. Our favourite species are the flag iris and the bearded iris, which seem ideally formed to attract their pollinators, with three beautiful sepals of vibrant colour spreading outwards and upwards, then three "falls" that drop downwards, often with elaborate speckled veins and freckles and a tufty little beard, which is in fact the pollen-laden filaments, making a perfect landing stage for bees. As the bee climbs deep into the flower to get to the deliciously fragrant nectar, it cannot help but collect the pollen as it reverses back out of the flower. The plant is ideally formed to make sure that the bee doesn't fertilize the same flower but deposits its pollen on the stigma of the next flower, as it blunders laden with nectar and pollen from one flower to the other, performing its most important role.

Irises have many uses, as well as delighting the eye and conjuring up myths and rainbows.

Some of the most beautiful irises of all were developed by the multi-talented artist and plantsman, Cedric Morris, who lived with his partner Arthur Lett-Haines at Benton End, in Suffolk. Morris and Lett-Haines moved in an artistic milieu and their friends included Barbara Hepworth and John Skeaping. They owned and ran the East Anglian School of Painting and Drawing, whose students included Lucian Freud, Joan Warburton, and Maggi Hambling. At Benton End, Morris began growing rare and exotic plants. He was most famous as a cultivator of irises, growing over a thousand species and producing over ninety new varieties in new and ravishing colour combinations. According to the great plantswoman Beth Chatto, his garden was a "bewildering, mind-stretching, eye-widening canvas of colour, texture and shapes." Cedric was also a talented artist, making many beautiful paintings of irises. You can visit Benton End and see the wonderful garden he created, and it is in the process of being revived as a centre for art and horticulture, too.

Irises have many uses. As well as delighting the eye and conjuring up myths and rainbows, the rhizomes, known as Orris root (*Rhizoma iridis*), have been used as a sedative medicine since ancient times; babies were given dry rhizomes to soothe their teething gums. Nowadays, this iris rhizome is not so commonly used in medicine but is still a popular basis for many perfumes and essential oils. The orris root is also used for flavouring gin. The well-known gin brand Bombay Sapphire uses the flower of *Iris germanica* for flavouring, and the lesser-known Magellan gin gets its sky blue colouring from the iris root.

How many times have you seen yellow irises at the edge of ponds and rivers? *Iris pseudacorus* is one of only two iris species native to the UK. They love to have their feet in a bog or water. They are also often planted there as part of a reed-bed system for purifying the water. The irises absorb pollutants and leave the water crystal clear, but if left to their own devices those rhizomes will just keep on multiplying and eventually clog the waterway. In some places where *Iris pseudacorus* has got out of hand, this beauty is considered a troublesome weed that needs to be culled. It is likely that the fleur-de-lys symbol of the French royal family is not, as usually imagined, a lily, but in fact a yellow iris from the River Lys.

We have made some lovely pressings with irises, but we have found it is better to choose delicate species. The little varieties from the group *Iris reticulata* or dwarf irises are best for pressing. The bearded irises are much more complicated, with their fibrous stems. Nevertheless, when you get a good pressing all the effort seems worthwhile.

Story

CORNFLOWER

When Howard Carter first entered the tomb of Tutankhamun in 1922, he found wreaths and garlands of cornflowers laid on the mummified body of the boy king. It is believed that the Ancient Egyptians had laid the flowers on the corpse to accompany him on his journey towards resurrection and eternal life. And there they lay, perfectly preserved for over 3,000 years.

According to legend, once a year the Nile would flood with the tears of the goddess Isis as she wept for the loss of her husband/brother Osiris at the murderous hands of his brother Seth. Osiris, the beautiful one, lord of love, king of the living and Eternal Lord, was brought back to life by Isis and

became a symbol of resurrection. In fact, the floods are due to Monsoon rains and melting snow in Ethiopia, far upstream. As well as water, sediment and silt is swept down the swollen river and deposited onto the arid desert land. When the waters recede, the land is left nutrient-rich and the crops can be sown. When the inundation did not happen, there was famine and great hardship for the people of Egypt.

To the ancient Egyptians this was an annual miracle. And with the arrival of the corn came its constant companion—the cornflower. The importance of the inundation in a land where rain never falls cannot be underestimated, so it is no wonder that the Egyptians came to believe the cornflower symbolized regeneration and used the flowers in the tombs of their Pharaohs to ensure their resurrection.

We know the cornflower is a very ancient decorative flower, too. There are depictions of it dating back to the fourth century BCE in Egypt. It can be found on wall friezes and in floor decorations, in pottery and faience. Cornflowers have even been found on necklaces, amulets and earrings dating back to the Armana period of 1364–1347 BCE.

The Latin name for cornflower, attributed to the flower by Carl Linnaeus, is *Centaurea cyanus*. He took the name from one of the many legends about the flower. When Achilles was mortally wounded by Hercules with a poisoned arrow, he was saved by the juice of the cornflower applied to his wound by a wise medic, the centaur Chiron. From here we get the *centaurea* part of the name. *Cyanus* simply means blue, from which we get the word cyan, and cyanotype or blueprint (see page 212).

Others may tell you that the cornflower was named for Cyanus, a handsome boy who loved the goddess Flora so much he did nothing but moon around in cornfields making garlands of cornflowers to lay upon her shrine. He was so in love that he forgot to eat or sleep and one day he was found dead in the fields, surrounded by the garlands he had made. His body was carried to the city of Florence, and Flora was touched by his devotion, so decreed the cornflower should bear his name.

Generally, cornflowers are a particularly lovely sky blue, although these days they can also be white, pink, several shades of blue, a deep plum, and almost black. Many artists have loved to paint the cornflower, particularly Sandro Botticelli. In his gorgeous pagan painting *The Birth of Venus*, the Hora of spring is waiting to cover Venus' nakedness with a rosy cloak embroidered with flowers. Hora herself is wearing a ravishing dress with a design of sprigged cornflowers. In Botticelli's *Primavera*, Flora is depicted wearing a garland and crown of spring flowers threaded with blue cornflowers.

A celestial fresco in the Bavarian Church of St Michael's, in Bamberg, depicts 578 wildflowers and herbs against a white background. The cornflower in one of the pendentives of the vaulted ceiling is most beautiful, and the whole ceiling is one of the finest botanical works of art I have ever seen. It served as inspiration for our pressed-flower wallpaper (see page 96).

It is hard to imagine that this innocent little wildflower was considered a pernicious weed for centuries and has been ruthlessly culled by farmers since the Middle Ages. There is evidence of cornflowers growing in the British Isles since the Iron Age, even then it grew prolifically among cereal crops, not only corn but also wheat, rye, and barley. It was considered a weed not only because it diminished the farmer's yield, but also because it blunted their scythes and sickles. In fact, one of its earliest common names is simply blunt sickle.

I was really shocked to learn that cornflowers growing in the wild in the UK have, through the use of pesticides and intensive farming, declined from 264 wild sites fifty years ago, to just three today. Now the few last sites where the flower grows wild are protected and conservation charities are working to bring it back from the brink of extinction. However, the good news is that as meadows of wildflowers become increasingly popular in city parks, on roadsides and on private land, the cornflower is not in any danger of disappearing anytime soon.

For such a little plant, the cornflower has an extraordinarily widespread influence.

This is important, because for such a little plant, the cornflower has an extraordinarily widespread influence. It is used as a symbol of many countries and institutions. It is the national flower of Estonia and the mascot of many Nordic political parties. It is beloved in Sweden where it has too many minor roles to even mention, but where it is a symbol for social liberalism. Queen Louise of Prussia, fleeing from Napoleon with her children, hid in a field of corn, keeping them quiet by making wreaths and crowns of cornflowers, and so after this the little blue flower became a symbol of Prussia. And it did go so nicely with the "Prussian blue" military uniform… After the unification of Germany, the cornflower became the symbol for the country. In Austria in the 1930s, it was a secret symbol worn by members of the illegal NDSAP party, which went on to become the Nazi party.

In France, the charmingly named "bleuet" is traditionally worn on Armistice Day out of respect for the victims of the Great War, just as we wear the poppy in the UK. Like the poppy, there was a proliferation of cornflowers after the ground was churned during that unholy battle. Meanwhile, in England the cornflower was the favourite flower of Edward Alleyn, founder of Dulwich College, where it is still the school's emblem—as it is for both the ancient schools of Winchester College and Harrow School.

Cornflowers serve other, practical purposes; they were used as a dye and as a medicinal herb for centuries, and they are edible, lending a charming and unexpected flash of blue to salads and desserts. If ingested they were supposed to improve your resistance to infections, cleanse the blood, purge the liver, and stimulate digestion, so they were often used in medicine as a diuretic and a mild laxative. An infusion of cornflower was also used as a remedy for tired and sore eyes. In France, cornflowers were long called *casse lunette* (break spectacles) because of their alleged magical healing properties for poor eyesight.

The other familiar name for the cornflower, "bachelor's buttons," came about because they were often worn as a buttonhole by young men in love—

including John F. Kennedy, who wore a cornflower on his wedding day, apparently as a tribute to his father Joe, whose favourite flower it was.

So what is it about this little wildflower? Is it a pernicious weed, a useful herb, or a symbol of tenderness and fidelity? Is it the symbol of the resurrection of the body and eternal life or the emblem of one of the most evil regimes in the history of the world? There are few flowers with such a very long history of symbolic importance.

Yet despite being the bane of farmers for so long and having such a chequered reputation, the cornflower has found its place in gardens today, including my own. For us, it is a little charmer. It is easy to grow and makes a beautiful pressed flower, with its slim, elegant wavering stems, which when pressed and preserved, allow us to imagine the flowers twisting and turning as the wind blows through the corn.

Story

MARIGOLD

In February 2017 I was travelling around India with Charlie, my husband. One morning we got up before dawn to go and visit the flower market in Kolkata. Something of a busman's holiday, you might think, but it couldn't have been further from what I am used to in New Covent Garden Market. The Kolkata flower market is crazy with colour; a collision of scents—delicious, spicy, human, and sometimes terrible. Then there is the noise: tinny, shrill music emanating from ancient transistor radios, dogs barking, the trundle of carts, shouting, spitting, hawking, and bartering. Tiny women carrying vast bundles of red roses on their heads, as they thread their way through the brightly coloured stalls. Everything is on a massive scale. Almost none of the flowers are in water, as they will all be sold before the sun is high.

Armfuls of fragrant tuberose and great bunches of colourful asters, sunflowers, and gladioli made up a lot of the cut-flower selection I saw, but what really impressed me were the coiled ropes of marigolds already made up into garlands; some simple and some mind-blowingly elaborate, with three differently coloured marigolds interwoven in intricate patterns. There were also huge, waist-high sacks filled with heads of orange and yellow flowers for those who wanted to make their own; deep-orange marigolds interspersed with white chrysanthemums, or threaded with jasmine for its exquisite scent. The slender fingers of the women weaving the flowers together with fine string are so deft that you just know however hard you tried, you could never make garlands like this. It's what they do, they learn it at their mothers' knees.

From Kolkata we moved on to Varanasi, the holy city on the banks of the sacred River Ganges, where Hindus go to die, if they possibly can, to escape the cycle of rebirth and attain Nirvana. We arrived at the train station at dawn, travel-stained and weary. The great Art Deco facade, with its sunburst motif, was, for the moment, home to thousands of huddled sleeping beggars, but as we climbed into our taxi and the sun rose through the cold foggy morning, they were being rudely awakened and moved on. Eventually our taxi driver deposited us and we began the slow crawl through the winding alleys to the Ganpati Guest House. Dragging our suitcases over the cracked paving stones and past the munching cows (cows are holy here and even the humblest household leaves snacks for them to graze on), we plodded through the cow shit and the grime, following our guide, bleary-eyed with lack of sleep. Then we became aware of sudden singing, chanting and bells approaching; we flattened ourselves against the wall, shaven-headed men rushed past us, carrying a gaudily wrapped corpse bedecked in orange marigolds on a stretcher held high. They were taking their loved one's body on its final journey to the burning ghats.

Calendula

The funeral pyres are on the banks of the great River Ganges, which is almost always shrouded in mist and smoke and looks like nothing so much as an eighteenth-century painting of Venice, or the Thames, by Canaletto. It is busy with wooden rowing boats and larger vessels bringing pilgrims from the other side of the river with elegant, pointed prows painted in lovely colours. On the steep steps of the ghats people bathe, pray, swim, and wash their clothes in the murky water. In his book *Being Mortal*, the author and physician Atul Gawande describes how he brought his father's ashes from the US to be scattered in the Ganges. He knew the rituals would require him to drink three teaspoons of Ganges water, and he also knew the dangers of doing so—many citizens of Varanasi have no access to running water and the river is an open sewer. Despite dosing himself with every antibiotic and preventative he could think of, he still became gut-wrenchingly ill. Yet you see the little children jumping off the boats and bridges, cheerfully swimming in the filthy water, or old men submerging themselves in their daily bathing ritual with no apparent ill-effects.

We cannot know how much hardship people have endured to take their loved ones to Varanasi to die, or what sacrifices have been made to hasten their souls to heaven. Certainly, the wealthy Rajahs all had riverfront palaces for the quick dispatch of elderly relatives. I often wonder how one might have felt when the family announced: "We were thinking of spending the spring in Varanasi this year." The one-way journey to eternal bliss. The hurried rush to the eternal fire; the marigold leis around your neck.

So in India marigolds are holy flowers. It would be gloomy if they were only the flowers of death, but they are also part of every celebration—marriage, birth, and all the religious feasts and secular festivals like Republic Day and Mahatma Gandhi's birthday.

In India, marigolds bedeck the shrines of the gods, they hang around the necks of pot-bellied Ganesh and fierce Shiva and curvaceous, many breasted Lakshmi. They adorn the bonnets of the brightly painted lorries ("sound your horn") and the doorways of grand houses and modest hippie huts on the beach. They swim serenely on basins of water in the finest hotels and palaces, which welcome you with fragrant incense and oil lamps as you are anointed on the forehead with a "tilak" of vermillion and turmeric and a lei of fresh flowers is hung around your neck. These ancient customs of welcome were originally for people of high status, because in India the guest is a god and must be treated with deference and ceremony. Nowadays, if you spend the extra dollar these customs are extended to you and me.

Marigolds have the good fortune of coming in just the right colours for religious ceremonies in India. Not many can afford saffron (handpicked stamens of the crocus flower) to dye their robes, but the marigold mimics the holy colours of orange, yellow, and maroon. It is not the national flower of India, though; that honour is reserved for the lotus flower. But when I think of India, that marvellous, maddening, jostling, vibrant, squalid, and crazily beautiful country, I always think of marigolds.

In India marigolds are holy flowers that are part of every celebration.

I have discovered that marigolds play just such a vital role in Mexico, too. Graveyards are colourful places, with graves often painted in bright colours and adorned with ceramics and photographs of the deceased. On 1 and 2 November, *Dia de Muertos*, or "Day of the Dead," people bring their deceased relatives gifts of their favourite foods and drinks, along with garlands of marigolds and other bright flowers to decorate their graves. They keep their lost ones company in an overnight vigil, telling stories and reminiscences. This tradition is a muddle between ancient Aztec rites and the Catholic All Saints' Day, or *Todos los Santos*. Over the past century this celebration has become increasingly commercialized, much like Halloween, but the sentiments of respect and love displayed by the Mexicans visiting the graves of loved ones—with their flowers and their oil lamps and the mariachis playing music through the night—is a beautiful thing. It's a far cry from our solemn, grey graveyards, although they have their beauty, too, but it must be hard to feel too gloomy beside a grave bedecked in brilliant orange and golden marigolds, eating tacos with a bottle of Mescal in your hand.

In Mexico, marigolds are called *cempasúchil* and are mentioned by a sixteenth-century friar, Bernardino de Sahagún, in his Florentine Codex, which documents the culture and customs of the Aztecs, even as they sought to replace them with Christianity. The marigold is noted by Sahagún for its important roles in both medicine and celebrations, and particularly Aztec feast days that honour the dead.

Marigolds are ridiculously easy to grow but they are also the most useful flower. Sometimes they seem almost too bright for our northern climate, but they really come into their own in the bright sunshine. Marigolds have many useful properties, according to herbalists the centuries over. The foliage has a musky scent and they are grown in vegetable gardens as companion plants to tomatoes, carrots, chillies, potatoes, and aubergines, to name a few—the pungent scent deters slugs and snails and pesky rabbits. Their usefulness in the garden does not stop here, as the nectar attracts pollinators like bees, butterflies, and beetles. Although when planting in your kitchen garden, note that brassicas do not like being grown too close to marigolds.

Sometimes marigolds are used as a poor man's saffron, because the rich orange-yellow colour of the florets is a useful food dye and is sometimes fed to chickens to make the yolks of their eggs more orange. Any foods that are traditionally yellow, for instance mustard, have often been helped along with the flowers of *Tagetes erecta*, or food colouring E161b.

Mexican marigolds (*Tagetes lucida*) have a mass of medicinal uses; it is very difficult to find an ailment for which an extract of the plant isn't useful. It seems to be efficacious in everything from lightning strikes to eczema. The leaves and flowers are edible and still in use in both traditional and modern medicine. They are used as an aid to digestion, as a diuretic and a narcotic, but also as a stimulant and, combined with peyote, as a hallucinogen. Other claims for its efficacy include a treatment for insect bites, sore eyes, and a hangover, and for use as an aphrodisiac. No wonder it was a firm favourite of the Aztecs, who made it into both tea and an incense called *Yauhtli*. The leaves have an anise flavour and it is used as a spice substitute for tarragon. Dried and burned, it is a useful insect repellent.

The name "*Tagetes*" comes from the Etruscan legend of Tages, who sprang from a deep ploughed furrow and taught the Etruscans the rudiments of farming and divination. Perhaps the name was given to the marigold because of its easy growing properties and how it springs back into flower from the stumps of the previous year's plant, or from the seeds it leaves in the ground.

Marigold, or "Mary's gold" in Christian myth, is the herb of the sun, representing—depending on the culture you believe in—purity, joy, good luck, grief, and surrender to whatever fate the gods have in store for you, and death and the resurrection of the body. Quite a lot of stories for such a humble, cheerful plant.

There are two distinct types of flower, both going under the familiar name "marigold." Both are from the Asteraceae or daisy family. The genera *Tagetes* and *Calendula* are kissing cousins; they probably both originate from South America, but today they are pretty much ubiquitous, as we can tell from their familiar names: French Marigold, Mexican Marigold, African Marigold. Calendula is a softer, less shouty flower, and much easier to use for the flower presser. If you can align the starry little heads neatly between two pieces of blotting paper, they can make a delightful pressing.

Project

SKETCH FACADE

In the early summer of 2018 we turned the entire facade of Sketch in Mayfair into a fantasy Rajasthani palace using dried and pressed flowers, which, considering it would have to survive the vagaries of the British weather, was our biggest challenge to date. Some of the most exciting, and often challenging, projects we've worked on have been commissioned by Sketch's creative director, Sylvain Chevelu. Sketch is an eighteenth-century Georgian townhouse, transformed by Mourad Mazouz into a series of eclectic bars and restaurants, serving as a platform for different designers and ever-evolving art installations.

Our first installation for Sketch was a hanging canopy of 6,000 flowers in the Glade bar in May 2016. After a week spent preparing and wiring all the flowers, we had a team of florists install everything over one endless night, everyone frantically attaching individual stems and bunches of foliage to cover a 40-square-metre (430-square-feet) wire mesh suspended from the ceiling. When we came to dismantle the ceiling, all the flowers were completely moisture-free, and with hindsight this was probably our first successful experiment with dried flowers. Despite the sky-high levels of anxiety in the making of it, the installation was deemed a spectacular success.

A couple of years and a couple more extravagant installations later, Sylvain gave us and a handful of other leading florists a curious brief: to create an installation based on a place or country of our choice; loosely related to the upcoming Royal wedding of Prince Harry and Meghan Markle and the places they might visit on their honeymoon. Melissa had recently returned from a month-long trip to Rajasthan with stories to tell and a phone full of images, so India seemed an obvious choice. Rather than basing our design on a specific place, our idea was to celebrate India and its relationship with flowers, including elements of a Rajah's Palace or a Hindu Temple.

The entrance to Sketch is a long corridor with arched alcoves set into the walls on either side of an extravagant gold-painted ceiling. Our proposal was to turn this space into a series of decorated doorways. Huge sacks and baskets of brightly coloured dried flowers would line the hall; rope leis of marigolds and carnations would hang from a framework covered in sari silk.

We began leafing through images of the exquisite heritage doors of Rajasthan; looking at the centuries-old carpentry work of the Suthar community, the abandoned palaces of Shekhawati and the interior doors at Udaipur's City Palace complex—a cluster of palaces built over 400 years ago, and a prime example of Mewari Rajput and Mughal architecture. In India, doorways are associated with cultural identity and new beginnings; they are framed by a series of elaborately carved and recessed arches, often painted and garlanded, while thresholds are embellished with traditional rangoli. A

GOUACHE
DALER ROWNEY
acrylic
burnt sienna
REEVES
Zhu Ting Artist Brush
rose leaves
rosebuds
24mm thick board
Colours :

Parlour
Salon de the
Patisserie
Breakfast
Brunch
Lunch
Tea
and
Cakes
take
them
here
or
take
them
away

rangoli is a colourful design made on the floor near the entrance to a house or temple using coloured rice powder or flower petals to welcome guests. These temporary decorative motifs are often used during Hindu festivals and later inspired our pressed-flower mandala.

Sylvain loved our visualization, but he decided that he wanted it realised on the facade of the building instead of the interior. This turned our idea on its head and into the ultimate challenge. It was mid-May, our busiest time of year, when everyone suddenly needs flowers. We had two weeks to transform the front of a four-storey listed Georgian building into an Indian palace.

To put this into context, in the two weeks leading up to the installation, alongside a handful of press events and our weekly flower contracts, we also had to install five weddings, a hanging ceiling of flowers for a private party, an enormous living floral arch for the front of a major London department store, a shop window display for Chelsea in Bloom, and make elaborate dried flower pieces for five Daylesford stores.

With this in mind, we were keen to design something that would be low maintenance, with few or no fresh flowers, because installations using fresh flowers demand a huge amount of daily care and attention and time that we just didn't have. Following our recent experiments with pressed flowers, we were excited by the possibilities of using them as a medium to make something spectacular.

While most Indian palaces are decorated with elaborate and colourful motifs on the inside, not the outside, we wanted the Rajasthani-inspired design to be instantly recognizable. Working out how to decorate the facade and not affect the paintwork or damage the fabric of the building, we decided to concentrate on the windows, designing decorative MDF surrounds to slot into the enormous window arches and the fanlight above the door. Just trying to get accurate measurements for the exterior alcoves was a challenge in itself.

This project was definitely ambitious, and wondering whether or not we could pull it off or not made for some sleepless nights. But once we had India on board, it began to take shape. With final measurements in hand only nine days before install, India spent hours drawing scaled plans and working out intricate patterns for the window surrounds, translating the elaborate painted motifs of these Indian temples into designs of pressed flowers set within painted borders.

Scalloped edges framed the windows looking into the parlour, while a semi-circular insert above the main entrance door echoed the panes of the fanlight behind. A series of seven decorated panels covered the planters running the length of the building at street level, featuring a giant central floral mandala made up of bright yellow daisies, tiny red rosebuds and pansies, flanked by scrolls of rose leaves and pressed flower heads.

With a hefty set build and a lot of work involved in the design, we needed to keep flower costs under control, so we had to use flowers that were readily available, quick to press, and relatively cheap to buy. Working on a huge scale with such tiny specimens, it was important to have repetition, so we

used delphiniums and larkspur to create many of the larger floral motifs. We placed clusters of delphinium heads with orange narcissi or pale yellow pansies in the centre to create fantastical flower heads. Butterfly ranunculus and burnt orange asters complimented the deep red paintwork. The abundant climbing rose growing in Melissa's garden was pillaged for its foliage, which we used as tracery throughout, with individual maidenhair fern leaves and tiny *Geranium renardii* flowers adding delicate detail.

The panels were built offsite and delivered in sections to our tiny studio, which was quickly taken over by a growing team of freelance artists and florists. Borders of royal blue, red oxide, and gold were handpainted before each individual flower head, petal, and leaf was meticulously glued down using a fine paintbrush. We used more glue to secure the flowers and added a layer over the top to protect them from the varnish topcoat. With no time to experiment, we used enamel sign-making paints and coated the whole thing in an outdoor varnish to ensure its survival in the elements. This was a worry, as we weren't sure how the varnish would affect the pressed flowers.

The decorative windows were made up of two sheets of MDF, allowing for circular cut-outs to hold dried flowers in relief, adding colour and texture to the design. Rows of statice in lilac and pale yellow, helichrysum in deep oranges and reds, and tiny rosebuds were stuck into place one by one with hot glue guns to make up these blocks of bright colour. The cut-outs were painted gold underneath to disguise any potential gaps, especially if a rosebud or two got blown away by the wind. The studio was chaos; rammed with people gluing thousands of tiny flowers into a sea of painted wooden panels perched on tables, plinths, and upturned flower buckets.

To bring this slightly eccentric idea together, we wanted to add some temple flowers to our fantasy palace. So we set off across London to Wembley to meet the utterly charming Sid from Jay & I Events, close to the Sanatan Hindu Temple—a florist with a magnificent set department who specializes in Indian weddings across the UK. There we discovered a treasure trove of giant Indian sculptures, life-sized painted elephants, gods and goddesses, lotus flowers, and papier-mâché mandaps—all the glorious paraphernalia of an Indian wedding. Melissa got overexcited and wanted to bring back a life-sized Indian elephant to stand at the entrance, but we managed to dissuade her and returned instead with two slightly more discrete Ganesh heads, which we placed at the top of our decorative windows. Ganesh is the elephant-headed Hindu god of new beginnings, who traditionally attends all Hindu weddings as the remover of obstacles and giver of good fortune; he often sits on top of the main door to offer protection and ward off any ill or bad luck entering the home.

Sid also supplied us with hundreds of marigold leis to stream down from the second floor. These were fake as we couldn't risk them going brown and dying, as they were extremely difficult to hang, so we threaded them with real dried flowers and sprigs of lilac limonium. They went to a very good home after the event, where they are still in use today. But we wanted real-flower garlands for the main entrance. Sid directed us to another

London-based florist called Mani from Valli, who specialize in garlands and flower jewellery for Indian weddings. We ordered a giant fresh flower garland to place over the door with two smaller ones to hang either side. It would have taken us weeks to create these incredible works of art, but for Mani and his team, it was all in a day's work.

At midnight we arrived with the large decorated panels to secure into the window and door alcoves, which lay beyond spiked railings and a long drop to the basement area. With clamps and stands and an uneven floor surface in the dark, it was quite frightening. The set builders ended up having to drill brass plates onto the wooden panels for support, which we reluctantly had to incorporate into the design. As the sun rose, our palace began to take form. And like all the best sets, it just needed to be in place before you could suspend your disbelief for a moment and be transported.

The final touch was filling the long exterior planter with brightly coloured salvias and African daisies (*Osteospermum*), which come in a whole range of electric colours in May to reflect something of the vibrant flowers of India.

The installation was supposed to be up for three weeks, but to our astonishment Sketch loved it so much they kept it up for the whole summer. Having made this as a temporary art piece we were constantly worrying about how long it would survive this extended exposure to sunlight with no UV protection. Despite being exposed to the full glare of the hottest summer on record and the occasional lashing of rain (this is England, after all), the panels were still strangely beautiful after three months. Although the colour had inevitably faded, we were impressed with how well the flowers had kept their shape and remained in place.

We would love to do something on this scale again now with our archive of larger pressed flowers and long curling strands of jasmine. There are a few other things we would have done differently, such as mixing the paint to try to capture the more chalky colour and texture of Indian pigments painted onto absorbent plaster walls rather than going for the safe option.

In the end, though, when we look back over our notes and consider the short lead time, we are amazed and delighted that we did it. We must have had nerves of steel back then! We know how lucky we were to have India, with her design skills and knowledge, and the tireless team of "*petites mains*" who helped us to bring the scheme to fruition. It remains one of our favourite projects, but only in hindsight. At the time it was plain terrifying...

Story

ROSE

I know a bank where the wild thyme blows,
Where oxlips and the nodding violet grows,
Quite overcanopied with luscious woodbine,
With sweet musk roses and with eglantine.
There sleeps Titania sometime of the night,
Lulled in these flowers with dances and delight.
And there the snake throws her enamelled skin,
Weed wide enough the wrap a fairy in.
A Midsummer Night's Dream, William Shakespeare (1564–1616)

A member of the family Roseaceae, the rose has over 300 species and many thousands of cultivars, with new ones being developed all the time. But let us start with our favourites and the easiest to press—the single wild roses that we find scrambling through the hedgerows in early summer: the dog rose (*Rosa canina*), sweet briar (*Rosa rubiginosa* or *eglanteria*), and musk rose (*Rosa moschata*). I think Titania, queen of the faeries in *A Midsummer Night's Dream*, chose this tangle of wild beauty to decorate her bedchamber not only for the gorgeous scent of the blooms, but also for their brambles and thorns. (Shakespeare's faerieland is a dark and sometimes frightening place, and vengeful Oberon was often in a rage!)

English roses, famous for their fragrance and their peerless beauty, are among some of the best in the world. Rose breeders like David Austin and Peter Beales worked tirelessly in their lifetimes to preserve many of the old varieties. They also created new cultivars, which combined the loveliness of the classic roses with the vigour, repeat-flowering form, and disease resistance of the newer species.

When I first became a florist I was quite disappointed by the roses in the market. The traders explained to me that many had been flown halfway around the world and that the scent and thorns had been bred out of them to give them longer life and make our job as florists easier. But there was also something rather sad about those straight, thornless roses, which lasted for an unnaturally long time then suddenly hung their heads without ever fully opening—so unlike the lovely garden friends that I remembered from my childhood.

When somebody brings you roses, your automatic reaction is to bury your face in an open flower to inhale its fragrance, so it is always a great disappointment to find them scentless. I have seen so many people lift their heads, bewildered, from such a beautiful bunch of flowers. Fragrance is often so interlinked with memory, so to deprive roses of their scent seems to take away something vital of their essence.

In the past ten years, it has become possible to buy beautiful, scented English roses from the flower market. Rosebie Morton, who founded the Real Flower Company in 1998, realized that there was a real desire among those of us who work with flowers for beautiful roses with scent and took action. She started her business with just sixty plants. When she took the first crop of roses up to London to offer them to florists, the reaction was entirely positive. Her flower business quickly grew into the great success it is today.

Of course, in England, the growing season for roses is very short—May through September, although there are always some fragile flyblown roses lingering until the first frosts. But the demand for roses doesn't stop when the summer is over, so we need to look further afield. I remember when somebody said to me, when I first became a florist, that it wasn't a very green business. I was amazed, what could be greener? I had so much to learn, we still do, but we are trying all the time to improve our practices.

Sometimes the right decision is not the apparently obvious one. I was excited to meet Maggie Hobbs from the Kenyan Flower Farm "Tambuzi." Located in the foothills of Mount Kenya, where the climate is perfect for growing roses, the farm is on the equator and gets an average of ten hours of sunshine a day and 800mm (31 inches) of rain a year, but it is also cool at night. The Hobbs employ 300 people, most of whom can walk to work each day, and they grow the beautiful scented roses that we all want to buy. I was fascinated to learn from Maggie that the roses grown at Tambuzi are actually far more eco-friendly than roses grown in Europe. Although they have much further to come, they weigh very little and are flown in the holds of passenger planes. In Europe, roses need heat, water, and light outside of their natural growing season, whereas in Kenya, these are all provided by nature. Tambuzi is proud to display the Carbon Neutral Gold Standard issued by the World Widlife Fund for the highest levels of environmental integrity and sustainable development benefits to local communities.

To deprive roses of their scent seems to take away something vital of their essence.

Perhaps the most famous pressed rose of all is one given by Hollywood legend Greta Garbo to Cecil Beaton in 1932. Beaton was staying with friends in LA when he was told that the famously reclusive Garbo was coming for dinner. He begged to join them as he had long admired her, but she refused to meet anybody new and he was told to keep out of sight. Beaton slipped upstairs, bathed and did his nails, then changed into white shoes and socks, a white kid jacket and "scanty little white sharkskin shorts." He came downstairs and entered the room where Garbo was chatting to his friends, whereupon he gasped, apologized, and made to leave. Of course, Greta was intrigued and he was invited to join them. The evening passed in a haze of mutual admiration. At some point, Garbo plucked a yellow rose out of a vase, kissed it and gave it to him. So began one of the strangest and most unlikely love affairs of all time. Both were bisexual, Cecil was a flagrant self-publicist and Greta shy and retiring. The affair was very much on and off with much teasing, advance, and withdrawal, but nevertheless it continued over many years. In 1975 Garbo came to visit him in his beautiful Queen Anne house in Wiltshire. Cecil was much diminished, having had a stroke the year before, and Greta announced she was glad she hadn't married him. Above his bed, framed and pressed, was the yellow rose, which he had placed between the leaves of his journal the night they met, forty years earlier. After his death the rose was put up for auction. It sold for £750.

There are many myths and legends about the rose; my favourite is the story of the infant Eros, who loved beautiful flowers. One day, burying his face in a rose in the garden, he was stung by a bee that was gathering nectar there. The aggrieved child rushed to his mother, Aphrodite, for comfort. She, perhaps irresponsibly, furnished him with a bow and arrows and urged him to take his revenge. The furious child fired off millions of tiny arrows. Many missed their mark and became lodged in the stems of the flower, and that is how the rose got its thorns.

Another more gruesome tale comes from Greek mythology. The goddess Gaia had many misshapen and terrifying children after she married her son Uranus. The Hecatoncheires were hideous, with 100 hands and fifty heads. Then came the Cyclops, who were equally monstrous—giants with one terrible eye in the middle of their foreheads. Uranus was ashamed of his monstrous offspring and locked them away in Tartarus, in the Underworld.

Still more children arrived: the Titans, who were not deformed but were unfeasibly enormous and strong. As soon as they were grown, Gaia set them against their father, charging them with the task of releasing her other children from Tartarus. Cronos, one of the Titans, cut off his father's genitals with a sickle and hurled them into the sea, where they stayed, surrounded in sea foam. Until one day, when Aphrodite emerged fully formed and very beautiful from the waves that broke on the shore. Where the wash fell, beautiful white roses grew. Later, Aphrodite tried to warn her lover, Adonis, that the boar he was hunting was actually the jealous god Aries in disguise. Tragically, she was too late. Adonis was killed. His blood ran and stained Aphrodite's roses red. There are morals to this tale: don't marry your mother! If you do marry your mother, don't have children. If you do have children, beware of ones carrying a sickle. And generally beware of angry children with castration on their mind…

Almost anywhere you travel in the world it seems like there are always roses, and they are part of the culture. More than any flower, they symbolize love and passion. The giving of roses seems weighted with symbolism, often a statement of intent, love, or regret. In Morocco they are used in medicine, for washing and in cooking; great sacks of tiny pink and red rosebuds are sold in the apothecaries in the souk. In the grander restaurants, rose petals are scattered on tables and in finger bowls. In Winston Churchill's favourite hotel, La Mamounia, in Marrakech, extravagant mountains of fresh roses are changed every day. In India, the palaces and temple gardens have brilliantly coloured roses growing out of the apparently impossible earth. In Mexico, the rose is predominant, adorning girls' hair in gardens and art.

Rose water is used far and wide, from cuisine to cosmetics to religious ritual. It is made by soaking rose petals in water, while rose oil is made by extracting the flower's natural oils. Both are used as a food flavouring, which is recognizable in delicious Middle Eastern sweets like Turkish delight.

There is evidence of the existence of the rose going back over 5,000 years in China and in Persia. In the famous rose fields of Qamar, near Kashan, the Iranian single rose is grown for its nectar. Roses are harvested at dawn when the nectar is extracted for rose water (called *goolab*). The rose appears in many Persian poems, and rose water mixed with saffron is often used as ink for writing poetry for extra inspiration.

For a long time it has been rumoured that King Henry VIII called Katherine Howard, his fifth wife, his "rose without a thorn," although I can find no evidence of this. Actually, Henry had many coins struck with the following motto: *HENRIC VIII RUTILANS ROSA SINE SPINA*, meaning "Henry VIII, a dazzling rose without a thorn," long before he met or married Katherine.

So it was Henry himself who was the rose without a thorn. Certainly, the rose was the symbol of the Tudor Dynasty, a bringing together of the white rose of the House of York and the red rose of the House of Lancaster as a sort of PR stunt by Henry VII to promote peace after the bitter civil war in England known as the War of the Roses (1455–85).

A relatively new trend among florists is to "reflex" roses by blowing warm breath onto the heart of the flower, then gently rolling back the petals to make them look more ravishing and abandoned. At JamJar we love the English garden roses, with overwhelmingly sweet fragrance. Their soft beautiful flowers don't last long and seem ready to fall apart voluptuously in your hands, but their fleeting beauty is unrivalled.

Pressing roses can be rather hit and miss, but if you select small spray roses like *Rosa banksia*, "ballerina," and "fairy" you will get beautiful results. We also love the exceptionally fragile *Rosa mutabilis*, which changes colour during its short flowering, endlessly putting up more pointed, pretty buds. Roses that open out to a flat shape and show their centres make the best pressings. Very stiff florists, roses designed for long life in the vase rarely do. If you experiment you will quickly find your favourites

Story

JOSEPH BANKS

It was in that strange time when the country first went into lockdown, in the spring of 2020, that we decided to write a book about flower pressing. Pressing flowers has been a practice for many hundreds of years; initially, perhaps, more as a matter of scientific record than as artistic expression.

Joseph Banks, the great eighteenth-century botanist, wrote instructions for pressing specimens for his team in 1770 and it is interesting to see how the methods we use have hardly changed in 250 years.

> When they are Brought home, which should be within a few hours after they have been gathered, they are to be put in between the leaves of a paper Book, two leaves of which should be left between each plant. They should be Layed (sic.) as smooth as they Conveniently Can, each leaf flat to the paper: but no leaves or flowers are to be pulled off even if they should happen to be Rumpled, the Books are then to be filed upon each other and a flat board or some such thing of 10 or 12 lbs Weight. Layed (sic.) upon them, to reap the leaves of the Books together, in this manner they are to lay 12 hours: they are then to be taken up and will be found damp, the plants must therefore be shifted into other Books that are dry, during which time they may be materially smoothed, and many leaves which have been Rumpled by the first laying in spread out flat and even.

Apart from using a lot of blotting paper and purpose-built presses, very little has changed in our process. Joseph Banks actually pressed many of his specimens between the uncut pages of a book called *Notes Upon the Twelve Books of Paradise Lost*, written by Joseph Addison in 1719. The irony of this was not lost on Mexican artist Jan Hendrix in his beautiful exhibition and catalogue "Paradise Lost," published in 2020. His work responds to the changing landscape of Kamay Botany Bay, in Australia. The contrast between the flora and fauna-rich countryside, which Banks described as "Arcadia" 250 years ago, with the still beautiful, but sadly depleted landscape of today, informs Hendrix's work. Sadly, much of the flora found by Banks when he first arrived with Captain Cook is now lost or vulnerable, a result of destructive fires and the ravages of climate change.

Joseph Banks (1743–1820) was an extremely wealthy and energetic young man with a passion for botany. After leaving Oxford, he decided to pursue this obsession, and so began an extraordinary career collecting and collating thousands of plants, which formed the basis for the collection at the Royal Botanic Gardens at Kew.

Unlike his privileged contemporaries, who puttered around Europe having fun collecting antiquities and commissioning artworks to decorate their

homes and plants for their gardens and hothouses ("Every blockhead does that"), the twenty-five-year-old Joseph Banks had loftier plans to go where no westerner had been before. He invested £10,000 of his own money—the equivalent of around two million pounds in today's monetary value—and by spreading it around liberally, and pulling as many strings as he could, he managed to secure himself a place on HMS *Endeavour* with Captain Cook.

King George III, affectionately known as Farmer George for his interest in all things agricultural and botanical, had commissioned Captain Cook to undertake a voyage to Tahiti in 1769 to observe the transit of the planet Venus as it crossed the sun. This was an important project that would enable scientists to determine the distance between the Earth and the sun which, in turn, would allow for the more accurate making of maps and charts.

The plan was to travel on from Tahiti, further south to find the fabled Terra Australis Incognita, and, if it was there, to stick a flag in it and claim it for the king. It was this part of the plan that interested Banks. An unexplored continent of new species was waiting for him.

The journey required a huge amount of preparation. His luggage included a large quantity of paper for pressing plant specimens as well as glass cases, boxes, and bottles for the collecting of plants; fishing tackle for marine species; and pistols, rifles, and ammunition. There were many other less obvious items listed that were deemed necessary for the comfort of a gentleman, including four servants, quantities of alcohol, apple pies, and a fine Cheddar cheese. On a later trip to Iceland he also took two French horn players, a chef, a gardener, a set of Wedgwood china, three liveried servants, and two dogs.

Despite these extravagances, we cannot underestimate the courage of these early explorers and the hardships they must have endured. A heart-rending page from Banks' diary in January 1771 describes his own illness and pain as he records the daily deaths of members of his team over the course of five days.

Accompanying Banks was the expert botanist Dr Daniel Solander, a pupil of Carl Linnaeus, who Banks greatly admired, and who had recently created a new system of documenting and classifying plants. Three artists were recruited to record the specimens they discovered: John Reynolds, Sydney Parkinson, and Alexander Buchan. Tragically, none survived the journey, all three dying of ship-borne illnesses. The greatest of these artists was Sydney Parkinson, whose exquisite and extraordinarily accurate work you can see today in Joseph Banks *Florilegium*, finally published in 1990, more than 200 years after his death.

Banks and his team were voracious plant collectors, amassing more than 30,000 plant specimens. Banks is attributed with discovering 1,400 new species previously unknown to the Western world, eighty of which are still named after him. He also brought tea from China and India; and so started the great British love affair with our favourite beverage.

Despite ingenious methods for keeping the plants alive, many were lost before they got home. The marvellously accurate botanical paintings, seeds, and pressed specimens were often all that was left as evidence of what they had found on their adventures. Banks was collecting plants so fast that he was in danger of running out of paper to press his specimens. At one point he arranged for 200 quires of paper to be taken ashore and spread out on a sail in the sun to hasten the drying process. We feel a lot of sympathy at JamJar, reading this story two centuries later and thinking of all the times we've tried to speed things up ourselves, with sunshine and microwaves, irons and electric heaters (not recommended!).

Banks was tireless in his foraging. As well as plants, he collected a thousand or more fish, birds, molluscs, insects, and other animals. He also "collected" a Tahitian expert navigator, Tupaia, and his girlfriend. Banks couldn't understand why he couldn't keep them "as a curiosity as well as my neighbours do lyons and tigers." In fact, tragically, Tupaia and Tayeto died of malaria in the East Indies. Today we view some of Banks' behaviour with considerable distaste; the high-handed way in which he and his contemporaries arrived in countries with no regard for the indigenous people, appropriating their lands, plundering their species and resources, and renaming their conquests after themselves is not to be celebrated; and his inhumanity in stealing people away from their homes and communities rightly appals our modern sensibilities.

The specimens remain beautiful and are a testament to the curiosity and determination of a man who sailed the world in a small wooden boat.

Upon his return to England, Banks found himself to be something of a celebrity. He housed his remarkable collections in a vast herbarium in his house at 32 Soho Square, where he generously allowed access to other botanists and scientists. He was elected president of the Royal Society in 1778 at the age of thirty-five, and remained in the position for the next forty-two years. He was also an advisor to King George III on the creation of Kew Gardens.

Banks was extremely knowledgeable but he never wrote papers, nor did he ever complete his eagerly awaited *Florilegium*, an illustrated record of his botanical discoveries on Cook's first voyage. He was, above all, a fixer, a networker, and a facilitator. He was generous with his wealth and well connected at court, with a world-wide network of naturalists with whom he shared his findings.

Specimens pressed by Joseph Banks and his team can still be seen at the Natural History Museum in London. Despite their loss of colour, the specimens remain beautiful and are a testament to the determination of a man who sailed the world in a small wooden boat to satisfy his insatiable curiosity.

Seen through the eyes of the twenty-first century, Banks was guilty of the kind of behaviour that is the cause of much that is wrong in the world today. But it is because of him and the wealth of species that he brought to our attention, along with the generosity with which he shared his findings, that Kew is the world's leading Botanical Garden. A centre of knowledge and learning, Kew addresses some of the biggest, most important issues facing all of us today—the loss of biodiversity, food security, and climate change—and owes thanks to the passionate botanists and explorers of centuries past.

Story

RANUNCULUS

Buttercups are just one of the many wildflowers that are part of the enormous Ranunculaceae family, which has over 600 species. Many members of the ranunculus family, like spearwort, marsh marigold, and crowfoot, are bog flowers. The word ranunculus in Latin means "little frog," and maybe that's because ranunculus, like the frog, likes to have its feet in damp places.

One of my earliest memories is of forcing back my brother's chin while he was in his pushchair and checking to see if he liked butter. The answer is that if it was sunny he did, and if it was cloudy he didn't. He certainly didn't love having his head rolled back by his bossy older sister. In fact, what he really liked were raisins dipped in fizzy lemonade and not much else. It is interesting to note that the reflective yellow petals are caused by layers of air trapped just beneath the surface, which causes the flower to act like a mirror bouncing the sun's rays back under the fat chin of the raisin lover.

There are many variants of the buttercup family, all of whom look very similar, the most common being *Ranunculus acris* and *Ranunculus repens*. They all contain a chemical called glycoside ranunculin, which when crushed turns into a blistering agent, which is why grazing animals will not eat buttercups and the flowers are able to thrive. Once tried by a young animal, never again. Fortunately, when meadow grasses and flowers are dried and turned into hay this agent is rendered harmless. The success of the buttercup in preventing itself from being grazed is also why it is considered a weed in some places.

Buttercups (*Ranunculus repens*) reproduce by their marvellous root system and once they have got a hold it can look as though the whole countryside is studded with gold. In fact, an old folklore myth tells that buttercups are fairy gold. A miser trudging through the fields with a sack of gold on his back was stopped by faeries who asked for one gold coin to roof a little house they were building. The furiously offended miser refused and the vengeful faeries cut a hole in his sack with a sharp blade of grass, and as the gold slowly emptied from his sack it turned into buttercups. The miser, noticing his load had lightened, turned back to see a meadow of dancing golden flowers and no gold left at all. And he could hear the faeries were laughing as they roofed their house with buttercups instead.

The Persian buttercup (*Ranunculus asiaticus*) originally comes from the Middle East and eastern Mediterranean regions. The first mention of it seems to have been when it was discovered by the crusaders in the Holy Land in the thirteenth century. These are the ranunculus we mostly use in floristry. Also known as turban buttercups, they arrive in hard little balls of brilliant colour on hollow stems, from deep purple through to reds, oranges, and yellow, and to pale pink and white. They are sometimes called coyote's eyes, as there is a rather unlikely legend of a coyote who threw his eyes into the air and caught them again, before an eagle intercepted and ate them. The coyote filled his blind sockets with ranunculus flowers. It is true that when closed they do have a little dark eye in their bulbous hearts, but leave them for a while and watch them unfurl, and their hard little green or black centres are revealed. A Persian legend has a young prince being so enamoured of a nymph that he sang to her night and day. The other nymphs became so irritated by the singing that they turned him into a ranunculus. In which case, I think he must have been very handsome.

Then there are the fancy ones, two-tone Moroccan varieties, and cappuccino ranunculus, which have little bitten edges as if someone had lightly dipped them into a pot of paint. Cloni Hanoi ranunculus are a particular

favourite of ours, which have enormous heads of tightly furled, papery petals that eventually open out into huge ballerina tutu heads. Cloni pon pon ranunculus are like the Moroccan variety, but supersized and elaborate. We love them all, they are all exquisite.

Ranunculus are also wonderfully reliable flowers with a long vase life. In fact, the flower becomes better and better in water, slowly unfurling its petals one by one until its magnificent head becomes too heavy for the stem, which then buckles under the weight. When this happens, we usually cut the stems and keep the flower heads going by propping them against the sides of the vase. The petals eventually become ethereally thin but continue long after the stem has withered and died. I know this because a few years ago I went to visit a friend who is an artist and whose mother had recently died. I wanted to take her some flowers, but all I had in the studio were some very open ranunculus in deep purples and oranges. I cut them low and clustered the heads together in a little mustard pot and set off for her big airy studio with its lovely north light. Six weeks later she sent me a photograph of them; they had collapsed in a most elegant and exquisite way. The water had all evaporated and the perky little buds now hung their heads as if in grief, but the original fully formed flowers had clung on to all their petals and exquisite shape and dried. And so they remained for a couple more years until Emma had to move studio. She tried to take them with her but they just crumbled into nothingness. I like to think they stayed with her through the long grieving process that we all must endure at the loss of a mother.

Ranunculus are often likened to mini peonies or complex roses, and many of the most exotic of the species were developed in Japan, where they are extremely popular. The tubers (or claws) can be bought and grown in the UK and in many temperate climates. They are not averse to cold conditions, they just don't enjoy frost and snow, so a period under glass or in a polytunnel is usually necessary.

Beautiful as they are, they are not much good for pressing. Or at least, they weren't until the magnificently talented Shuichi Kusano of the AYA Engei Nursery in southern Japan brought us our almost top favourite flower to press—the butterfly ranunculus (*Ranunculus rax*). This variety is more like its cousin the buttercup, it has the same iridescence in its high-gloss petals, but it is bigger and flashier and comes in a variety of gorgeous, burnished colours.

So, for the pressers among you, we do most highly recommend some of the members of the enormous ranunculus family for the craft. Especially the humble buttercup, which you can find beside the road and in fields and meadows throughout the English summer, and its very sophisticated cousin the butterfly ranunculus, which you can buy from good nurseries to grow your own, or you can purchase stems from fine florists everywhere.

Story

OSHIBANA

The use of pressed and dried flowers as a medium for creative expression seems to have begun in Japan in the sixteenth century; although it is possible it was an even older craft imported from China. The art of creating pictures using pressed flowers and plants was practised by Samurai warriors as part of their training in patience, concentration, and the importance of being in harmony with nature.

The Samurai were a caste of fearless and noble warriors, who were as well versed in arts and culture as they were in strategic and military skill. Immensely important and powerful, they ruled over Japan from the eleventh to the mid-nineteenth century. They were a ruling military class who lived in fortified castles, often surrounded by beautiful gardens. They were extremely self-disciplined, apparently indifferent to pain, and their obedience and loyalty to their masters was exemplary. Their symbol was an exquisitely crafted sword; the Samurai wore two swords and their skill with weapons was equalled only by their excellent penmanship. They were expected to achieve a fine balance between "the bun and the bu"—the arts of war and peace.

One of the more unpleasant practices of the Samurai was the art of "*Tsujigiri*," or "cutting down at the crossroads," where they tested the sharpness of their sword by randomly beheading an innocent passer-by on the roadside. Warriors were expected to be "a complete man," equally expert in the teachings of Confucius and Zen Buddhism as they were in the art of war. They practised arts more often associated with monks than with soldiers. They were well versed in "Chado," the "Way of Tea," an elaborate tea ceremony imported from China, and also studied poetry, calligraphy, watercolour painting, monochromatic ink painting, rock gardening, and Noh theatre. Based around Buddhist themes, the Noh plays involved ornate clothes, exquisite masks, and music.

It is difficult for us to equate such fierce warriors with a gentle craft like Oshibana—carefully pressing and placing petals into intricate designs. I love the idea of these splendid creatures in their exquisite garb, setting their weapons aside and settling down to an hour or two of pressed flower art.

If you google "Samurai warrior" today the first ten entries are for a "hack and slash" video game based around the Sengoku period in Japanese history. Though Samurai still have a resonance today, I suspect it is more for the "bu" than the "bun."

There are many artists who still practise Oshibana in Japan, but the word has become a sort of generic term for flower pressing in general.

八幡大菩

Story

LILY

For sweetest things turn sourest by their deeds
Lilies that fester smell far worse than weeds
"Sonnet 94," William Shakespeare (1564–1616)

When Zeus brought Hercules—his enormous son, conceived with a mortal woman—to his wife, the goddess Hera, to be suckled while she slept, she, not unreasonably, awoke and pushed the imposter away. The divine milk from her breast spurted forth into the sky, creating the Milky Way, and where the drops spilled onto the ground, fields of the first pure white lilies grew.

The birth of the lily in Greek and Roman mythology is a melodrama all tied up in the rape of Hercules' mother, Alcumene, by Zeus, and the violent jealousy that followed. The story first features Hera, who has been betrayed, then Aphrodite, who, arising fully formed and beautiful as the day from the sea, spied a lily and was so envious of its perfection that she caused the phallic pistil to grow from its pure white heart.

Perhaps that is why the lily is such a complicated flower; worshipped for its purity and beauty on the one hand, and reviled for its strong perfume and unseemly pistil on the other.

Many of us are conflicted by our feelings about lilies; they last brilliantly well as a cut flower, being showy and reasonably cheap to buy, but the thick coating of pollen on the anthers causes heinous stains and the tremendously strong perfume fills some people with dread, others with sneezes, and still others with rapturous delight.

In Christian mythology, the lily represents not only the Virgin and her chastity, but also the Crucifixion and the purification of the soul. In almost every Renaissance depiction of the Annunciation, when the Virgin Mary is visited by the Angel Gabriel to announce that she is pregnant with the son of God, the angel is almost invariably holding a lily, the symbol of Mary's purity—it is also the emblem of Florence, city of flowers, where most of the paintings were commissioned by the Medicis or other rich patrons. The Angel Gabriel is almost always depicted on the left and the Virgin on the right, and often there is a pot of lilies between Gabriel and Mary. I would tell you the apocryphal story of the pot of miraculous lilies, but it is rather dull. Let us just call them miraculous.

Much more interesting are the five remaining mediaeval examples of the lily crucifix in the UK. Nobody seems to know much about these rare depictions, or why Christ is depicted crucified upon a lily. Possibly it came from a belief that the Annunciation and the Crucifixion happened on the same day (in different years), and the lily represents the purity of the Virgin Birth and the resurrection of the soul.

It is believed there were once many more lily crucifixes that were lost during the Reformation, when Henry VIII had "idolatrous" religious art destroyed as he broke away from the Church of Rome and established the Church of England, with himself at its head. In the Parish Church in Godshill, on the Isle of Wight, there is an exquisite example of a lily crucifix. This beautiful, fragile image was whitewashed over by the clever Catholics during the dissolution of the monasteries, to protect it, then forgotten about. It was only revealed again in 1842 during restoration work. The lily is present in so much Christian iconography. Lilies even have Christian familiar names—the Madonna lily (*Lilium candidum*) and Easter lily (*Lilium longiflorum*)—my personal favourite, with its long, elegant trumpet flowers.

There is a strong connection between lilies and death and funerals, which may be why the perfume evokes such hatred and dislike in the hearts of its detractors. Maybe the lilies' connection with funerals might also have something to do with their strong scent masking the odour of death.

The scent of a lily weaves a devious path between delicious and disgusting. Anyone who has emptied the water of two-week-old lilies will know how terrible an experience it can be. Sometimes you can walk into a room after a hot day when the windows are closed and it will be pregnant with the scent of lilies, with something much worse hovering beneath the sweet fragrance. (Change the water and drop half a baby sterilizing tablet into the vase to help counteract this). When the first lily flowers have died, leaving the chaos

The scent of a lily weaves a devious path between delicious and disgusting.

of messy stamens and pulpy flesh hanging from the stem, a new bud opens perfectly pure and fresh, so there are two assaults on the nostrils: the sweet notes of the unfurling bloom above the noxious stench of death.

In short, the lily represents chastity and death and the purification of the soul to Christians, but to the Assyrians and Babylonians it represents the goddess of fertility, Ishtar. In Roman myth, through Venus and the satyrs, the lily represents lust. In Greece, brides wore garlands of lilies in their hair to depict a life of fruitful purity. In China, lilies are a symbol of good luck, frequently used in weddings because they symbolize 100 years of love. In Buddhism, the orange tiger lily represents mercy and compassion. In France, the fleur-de-lys, a stylized version of the lily, represents royalty, nobility, and grandeur. Florence, the city of flowers, is also represented by a fleur-de-lys, but unlike the French version, this lily has stamens. And anyway, it is said that the French fleur-de-lys is not a lily at all, but a yellow iris from the River Lys (see page 144). See? I told you this flower was complex.

Then there are all the flowers that call themselves lily but aren't really, like the water lily or lotus flower, or the lily of the valley, or the Peruvian lily — also called alstroemeria, but we are not going down that particular rabbit hole today. This is the story of *Lilium*, a genus of herbaceous flowering plants that have an important role to play in the culture and literature of much of the world. Definitely complicated to press, because their waxy petals are slow to dry, as we discovered, but too fascinating not to have their story told here and when you become more skilled and with a little perseverance they can make really gorgeous pressings.

Project

DECORATING FURNITURE

Amy and I arrived at Kempton Antiques Market before the sun was up. The early birds were in search of worms. Our breath steamed in the frozen air as we hurried for the tea stand. In the rosy light of dawn, other bargain hunters emerged and surged onto the racecourse looking for treasure. On our list were big glass vases, interesting and unusual containers that could be converted into vases, and lots of poison bottles in green, blue, and amber to replace the frequently broken ones that line our studio window. I also needed something to store documents in my tiny writing room.

A little cupboard caught my eye, someone had gone to some trouble to elevate it a little from the usual piece of jumble. I liked the zinc trim, the French grey paint and the good drawer knobs. It was £40. We didn't bother to barter, just peeled off a couple of notes and popped it into the back of the Jam Van.

Much later, India and I drove down to Thyme, in Gloucestershire, to do a flower-pressing course. Before the clients arrived we went down to the water meadows to collect some wildflowers. The meadows were ablaze with waist-high buttercups and we filled three or four presses. On our drive back to London I said to India, "I have this little grey chest at home and I have an idea for the buttercups."

We laid the chest on the cobbles in the yard and I gave the battered edges a quick lick of paint. Buttercups have a special luminescence and yellow on the grey is a winning combination. We started to lay out the flowers. We decided to decorate the drawers and the door panels, leaving everything else clear. We messed about with some other flowers but, as usual, we found keeping it simple and sticking to Plan A was best. The picture I had in my mind of shiny yellow buttercups dancing on a grey background began to take shape.

We used our favourite glue, Mod Podge, to fix the buttercups onto the drawers, painting a thin layer over the flowers as a sealant. When everything was completely dry we added another coat of matte varnish for protection.

The modest little chest was transformed. It looked beautiful, ethereal, magical. When it was safely installed in my writing room I decided I had to find a better purpose for it than hiding all the boring paperwork.

TIP: Lay out your design carefully and photograph it before you start the gluing process so you have a reference for placement. Use markers to remember where each stem was as you remove it for gluing—masking tape or pins are handy for this. If applying varnish, brush in one direction with a wide, flat brush to ensure an even finish. If you are applying flowers to a tabletop it is wise to get a piece of glass cut to size to lay over the top to protect the flowers.

Story

CARNATION

Sir. Kindly allow me to contradict, in the most emphatic manner, the suggestion, made in your issue of Thursday last, and since then copied into many other newspapers, that I am the author of *The Green Carnation*. I invented that magnificent flower. But with the middle-class and mediocre book that usurps its strangely beautiful name I have, I need hardly say, nothing whatsoever to do. The Flower is a work of Art. The book is not.
Oscar Wilde, letter to the Pall Mall Gazette, 2 October 1894

Never has a flower suffered from the vagaries of fashion more than the carnation. Beloved of the Victorians, it was grown in the hothouses of the great estates for elaborate table decorations. Then in the early twentieth century it reached an absolute fervour of admiration when Cecil Beaton photographed the young Princess Elizabeth in an elaborate bower of chrysanthemums and carnations, and Queen Elizabeth, the Queen Mother, in a dress covered in frills and sparkles, festooned in more carnations. Soon after this, there was an unseemly rush of debutants getting their photographs taken in a similar style. With flowers. Except who can successfully pull off these Beaton extravagances except the master himself?

My own mother's wedding bouquet in 1949 was a Beaton-style wide spray of carnations, roses, and asparagus fern. Then just as suddenly as it was popular, the carnation dropped from grace and became almost reviled. I sometimes think this is because it is almost ridiculously cheap and easy to grow. Its reputation was not, in fact, helped by the flower's reliability and longevity; sprays of red carnations nestled in some Babies' Breath (or *Gypsophila*) hanging around for far too long in the forecourts of garages or sitting limply in supermarkets have not helped their reputation. This particular combination sets my teeth on edge. What is it about red and white flowers that make them so rarely work together? Blood and bandages perhaps?

Recently we have noticed that the carnation is creeping back into fashion—and why not? At its best it is a beautiful flower with a complex petal structure and a most delicious, unusual scent with a strong hint of clove. We love the delicate, fragrant, white spray carnations and there are many new cultivars with beautiful subtle colouring in shades of knicker-pink, apricot, and beige, which we have come to love. Sometimes, annoyingly, they are called "vintage," that overused word, when they are actually brand new species. See, for instance: "Antique Prince Charming," "Vintage Candy Cane," or "Dusty Pink." In these subtler tones, a far cry from the gaudy supermarket favourites, the carnation is wheedling her way back into favour again.

Carnations (*Dianthus caryophyllus*) are sometimes called clove pinks, and pink is definitely their original colour. Some suggest the name "carnation"

comes from the Latin "*carnis*," meaning "flesh" (which is, of course, pink). But I prefer the explanation that the name originates from the Latin "*corona*," meaning "crown" or "garland." As a florist, I know the carnation makes excellent garlands, hair crowns, and, of course, buttonholes, for they are easy to wire and are robust for long periods of time out of water.

The carnation's original home is Greece, Italy, and the western Mediterranean. It is from here that one or two of the many myths that surround this flower arose. One story goes that the goddess Diana (or Artemis), the huntress, fell passionately in love with a young shepherd boy, who spurned her. The vengeful goddess then plucked out his innocent eyes and hurled them to the ground, where carnations immediately sprang up. Or was it that she was annoyed because he (the shepherd boy) was playing the flute and disturbed her prey while she was hunting so she ripped out his eyes? Yet another myth is that Zeus was so jealous of Hera and her lilies that he wanted a flower of his own and, being a furious fellow, he threw down a thunderbolt onto the plain of Thessaly, where the carnation was born. The Christians, without much imagination, have the carnation growing where the Virgin Mary shed tears as her son carried his cross to Calvary.

Duller than dull are the meanings for the different-coloured carnations: red for passion, white for purity, yellow for jealousy… I won't go on, I think you have got the gist.

Oscar Wilde loved to wear a rare green carnation in his lapel, and for that reason the green carnation has come to symbolize homosexuality and, I think, courage, because Oscar Wilde was a very courageous man as well as a talented one. His downfall was being too entertaining for his own good. His flamboyance—green carnation and all—his flagrant homosexuality at a time when it was a criminal offence to be gay, plus his pride and inability to resist the desire to be witty in court when he decided to take on his lover's angry father, the Marquess of Queensberry, all contributed to his undoing. He thought he could win both the case and the stony heart of his young lover, Lord Alfred Douglas.

In the event, he could not do either. His conviction earned him a long spell with hard labour in jail, and Wilde, who had lived the luxurious life of a successful celebrity playwright and author, the darling of society, could not cope at all with his reduced circumstances. He became very ill in jail and died, penniless, in France, in a room with loathsome wallpaper, shortly after his release. The green carnation seems to symbolize all that was folly in Oscar Wilde and a lot that was great.

During World War II, Prince Bernhard of the Netherlands took to wearing a white carnation, which came to symbolize the resistance and defiance of the Dutch people against the Nazis. Since the war, the white carnation has been worn in Holland to honour the prince and the veterans and in remembrance of the resistance, rather as the UK has adopted the poppy to remind us of the appalling sacrifice of young men's lives.

On 25 April 1974, in Lisbon, Portugal, a military coup overthrew the authoritarian Estado Novo regime. Thousands of civilian demonstrators joined the military in the protest against the right-wing government, and among them was a waitress called Celeste Caeiro. Celeste worked in a brand new restaurant that had planned to give carnations to all of its customers on its opening night, but, due to the uprising, the restaurant was closed and Celeste was allowed to take the unwanted carnations home with her. She offered her flowers to the soldiers in the street, who placed the carnations in the muzzles of their guns and in their buttonholes. Local florists soon followed suit and in no time the soldiers and the tanks and weapons of war were covered in carnations. Portugal became a democracy that day, with hardly a shot fired. The coup became known as the Carnation Revolution. Today, the *Dia de Liberdade* on 25 April is still commemorated with carnations. Flower power working at its best.

If after all this you are still not feeling the love for carnations, you only have to look again at the Dutch still life paintings of the seventeenth century to see why they are, and were, so beloved. For example, try *Still Life with Carnations and Exotic Fruit* by Jan Van Os (1744–1808) or *Flowers in a glass bowl* by Rachel Ruysch (1664–1750). These paintings remind us why carnations are beautiful and necessary. The classic carnation is not so great for pressing—having a large juicy receptacle—but select those more delicate garden varieties, like the two-toned dianthus seen here, and you will get beautiful results.

Project

ROSA BANKSIAE TRIPTYCH

For an exhibition we were working on in the spring of 2021, we had an idea to use one type of flower to make a triptych—a rambling or trailing plant going through three different frames that are linked together and designed to be hung side by side. Remembering that my friend Suzy had a particularly fine *Rosa banksiae*, we made a phone call to see if we could beg, borrow, or steal a few long branches for this piece, which we had been thinking about for a while. *Rosa banksiae* is always the first rose to bloom, but she was particularly late this year. A long, dark, freezing March followed by an April drought meant that the plant was behind last year by about three weeks, but on 28 April Suzy called and said the rose was ready for us to come and take some branches.

When we cut the branches, we were looking for long stems with buds at the ends and an interesting shape. We didn't want woody stems that would be too thick in the press. We were looking for new growth and flowers in bud as well as fully out roses. Suzy's daughter Lily climbed along a narrow wall to cut the best pieces while I stood and pointed and shouted on the ground. (Apparently, that's my strong suit—the pointing and shouting!)

I took the branches back to the studio for Amy and I to press. We used extra-long presses that our downstairs neighbour in the yard crafted for us out of offcuts from our MDF studio shelves. He drilled eight holes, four a side, to take extra-long screws. These giant presses are great for a piece like this and very easy and cheap to make, and MDF doesn't tend to warp as some other types of wood do.

We pressed the branches by considerably thinning out the flower heads so that each of the tiny rosebuds was lying flat on the page. The leaves are almost as beautiful as the minute yellow roses, so we made sure we pressed lots of extra leaves. We also pressed the flowering sprigs we had cut out so that we could add them into the finished piece as extra detail, if required.

It took about three weeks for the roses to completely flatten out and dry. We changed the blotting paper a couple of times to be extra sure nothing was rotting, but when we finally opened the press we found the *Rosa banksiae* had behaved just as well as she had done the year before. The roses seem to press very prettily, with elegant lines and dark edges on the little buds.

Laying out the flowers is where I cease to be useful. I can see exactly how I want the artwork to look, but the meticulous accuracy that Amy and India apply is just not my thing. I am too messy and impatient. I hurry things. I watch as my co-conspirators compose the piece, it is a fiddly business. First, they go through each individual pressing to make a selection of the most beautiful shapes. They lay out each branch, allowing one to flow into the

next, trying lots of different layouts until the spacing and flow feels elegant and balanced. Once they're happy, they cut the stems at the point where the board ends and lay the rest of the branch on the next page. It takes a long time to lay out a piece like this. The placement of the plant must feel natural, there must be a flow and consistency to the sprays of the rose as they meander from one board to the next, as if they are growing through the frame of a window. Eventually, when finished, it should look as if those beautiful arches are blowing in the wind. It should remind you of the end of April when the sun begins to gain some warmth and everything is growing. Yellow is the colour of spring and nobody does yellow as beautifully as Miss Rosa Banksiae.

When we had all agreed on the final composition, each component was taken off individually to be glued, but not before the position of the placement had been marked out with the help of pins with little coloured heads. This meant we could be sure that when the roses were laid back on the mount board they hadn't moved from their original position. This exacting practice is most important on a triptych, because the rose must look as if it is

naturally flowing from one piece to the next—even a few millimetres out can break the harmony of the finished piece.

Once all the flowers were glued down—another long and careful process—we stood back and were delighted. There is a lovely soft swaying quality to the piece; an April breeze is apparently blowing and the little yellow roses are dancing joyfully in the soft air. Everything was then packaged up to go to the framers. In this case we used a very simple, slim, black aluminium frame to add a definite line to the edges of the pieces. We wanted the three artworks to feel airy and feather-light. As usual, it was framed with museum glass with a UV filter to prevent the flowers fading too quickly. But even when it does inevitably fade it will continue to be beautiful, as this design relies heavily on the shape and structure of the plant. The colour, although lovely, is not the focus at all.

TIP: Other flowers that make a stunning triptych would be nasturtium, sweet pea on the vine, jasmine, and various climbing clematis—if you can catch them before they have twisted and entwined around themselves.

Story

BOTANICAL HEROINES

It is hard to remember that, up until the twentieth century, the opinions of women were considered irrelevant in any intellectual or scientific areas. Some women finally got the vote in the UK and Germany in 1918 (although women in the UK did not have equal voting rights with men until 1929), Holland and Austria in 1919 and the US in 1920. French women did not get the vote until 1944, and in Greece it was 1952. That's two years before I was born! For the preceding centuries women were supposed to only involve themselves in the running of the home, after that, if they were remotely well born, they had little more to do than read, draw, or paint, sing, play instruments, speak French, and make exquisite embroidery. They were largely uneducated and their opinions counted for little; essentially wives were considered, in both law and practice, to be the chattels of their husbands. Unmarried women had to remain at home with their parents and act as unpaid carers. There were, therefore, few opportunities for women to express their intelligence, should they want to do so.

Botany was one of the areas where a woman could slip through the back door and into the world of science. What could be more innocent-seeming than a woman picking and pressing flowers from the garden and creating pretty picture books? Here are some stories of a few of the ladies who used the flower press, or botanical exploration, as an outlet for their creativity and scientific curiosity, and a way out of the limitations imposed on them by their sex.

MARY, DUCHESS OF BEAUFORT (1630–1715)

"When I get into the storys of plants I know not how to get out."

I love this quote from Mary, Duchess of Beaufort; when I read it, I knew exactly what she meant and felt an affinity that spans the 400 years separating us. I wish I had known her, with her skill, knowledge, and enthusiasm to learn. I feel a great respect for her and all her achievements. Mary was, by all accounts, a formidable woman, with a passion for gardening, botanical study, and raising plants, that was quite exceptional for the time. Twice-widowed and the mother of eight children, many of whom predeceased her, she suffered quite severely from depression. Her curiosity and love of botany and gardening was a comfort and a solace, as well as a serious intellectual pursuit. Unlike many of the ladies who created herbaria, Mary was also a keen gardener, with an impressive knowledge of plants and a great skill in getting them to grow for her. In the seventeenth century, most scientific discoveries and exchanges took place in the coffee houses, clubs, and societies from which she was excluded, by virtue of her sex, yet she was extremely well considered by her contemporaries, entering into correspondence with all the great naturalists of her time, with whom she exchanged ideas, seeds, and knowledge.

She found her joy and an outlet for her intelligence in the gardens at her homes at Badminton and the enormous Beaufort House on the banks of the River Thames in Chelsea. The latter being close to the Chelsea Physic Gardens, where she was one of the first people to use a heated glasshouse to raise the many plants and seeds given to her by plant explorers from their travels around the world. The head gardener in the hothouse at Badminton was, very unusually for the time, a woman, known only as Mary or Martha.

The Duchess of Beaufort made an extensive herbarium to record the plants she loved. During her long life she produced twelve volumes of pressed and dried plants, which she bequeathed to Sir Hans Sloane, who, in turn, left them to the National History Museum, where they are now housed. She also commissioned an extensive catalogue—or florilegium—of paintings of her prized exotic plants, which remains in the library at Badminton House.

Mary kept extensive notes (or "storys") about her plants; she noted where they came from, whether they thrived or did badly, and although her work was undertaken as a serious scientific study it is also a thing of great beauty. She often included pressed butterflies and insects to add charm to the composition of each page. The herbarium shows this was not only a scientific pursuit but an artistic one, from which she gained pleasure and satisfaction.

The Duchess of Beaufort was, of course, a very privileged woman with the wealth and influence that allowed her to pursue her hobby and gave her access to the most eminent botanists, but she, nonetheless, turned that hobby into serious and respected scientific work.

An example of how even a woman of a great family was considered unimportant and of no value occurred when she attended the trial of a Catholic barrister, during the Popish plot. Her presence was objected to by William Bedloe, who was an informer and a man she despised and trusted no further than she could see him. Bedloe's objection was based on the fact that she was taking notes of his evidence. The judge dismissed his concerns, saying she could write whatever she wanted as nobody would pay any attention anyway, "no more than her tongue, truly."

Mary, Duchess of Beaufort, suffered no fools; she had a sharp and articulate mind, as we can see from her correspondence. She overcame her own melancholic disposition through hard work and the eager acquisition of knowledge, but perhaps the plants she pressed are the most articulate expression of her creativity and eye for beauty.

MARY DELANY (1700–88)

Mary Delany, neé Granville, was born in 1700. Her family, relations of Lord Lansdowne, were gentile, but impoverished and Mary, an extremely bright child, was sent to live with a childless aunt in the hope of eventually finding her a place at court. After the death of Queen Anne, these hopes were dashed and Mary was married off, aged seventeen, to the drunk and decrepit sixty-two-year-old Alexander Pendarves, who lived in a crumbling castle in Cornwall. It is hard to imagine now how powerless she must have felt, or how grim her prospects must have seemed, as she embarked on the long journey to Cornwall with her new husband. Mary's first piece of luck came when she woke up and found her husband "quite black in the face" and not breathing in bed beside her. As a widow she could now respectably go out into the world, but her husband had left her penniless, having omitted to alter his will on their ill-fated marriage, so she was still dependent on the kindness of others.

Mary spent her time moving between the homes of friends and relatives; but with her extremely lively mind and great perception she was a popular guest, and she was soon taken up by the Duchess of Portland, who introduced her to Joseph Banks. Banks gave Mary access to his herbarium, where she was able to spend long hours. She was particularly delighted by the exotic plants. Her great love of gardening and botany flourished under his tutelage; she was also a talented artist and needlewoman, both pastimes being considered perfectly respectable for women at that time. On a visit to Ireland she met Patrick Delaney, a married vicar, with whom she struck up a great friendship over their shared love of nature. When Delaney's wife died, he asked Mary to marry him, so at the age of forty-three she finally gained independence from the kindness of friends and embarked on a very happy marriage. The Delaneys lived in Ireland, where they created a beautiful garden and Mary continued her shell work and needlework, all inspired by her love of flowers and plants. After twenty-five years of marriage, Patrick Delaney died, leaving Mary a widow again, aged sixty-eight.

It was not until she was aged seventy-one that Mary started on the work for which she is still famous to this day, and will be for centuries to come. Finding a fallen geranium petal the exact colour of a piece of paper, she was inspired to make her first mixed media collage of a flower. She called them her *Mosaiks*, 985 life-sized botanical masterpieces that can now be seen at the British Museum. As well as paper, which she coloured with pigments, she also incorporated the actual parts of the dried pressed plants in her compositions.

Her work was informed by the dissection of plants that she carried out herself for complete botanical accuracy. By carefully layering minute pieces of hand-painted paper of different thicknesses and shades, she built up her collages of the petals, calyx, leaves, stamens, and sepals until she had reproduced the whole plant. Setting them on a black background made her work rich and vibrant, something that inspired us to try black as a background for our own pressings. She only stopped working at the age of eighty-eight, when her eyesight failed her.

Mary was a great favourite of King George III and Queen Charlotte, who gave her a small pension and a house on the Windsor Estate, from where she taught the royal children about botany and instructed them in needlework. Although Mary will always be remembered for her decoupage, she was also a fine embroiderer, and her subject was always botanically accurate flowers, which she rendered with exquisite skill.

She is included in our list of women flower pressers because she quite frequently included dried or pressed elements of plants in her collages, but also because, despite the limitations on women in her time, she rose to being a favourite in court purely through her sharp wits, sense of humour, and talent. A far greater achievement in the eighteenth century than it would be considered today. Her work is now housed in The Enlightenment Gallery at the British Museum and one of her embroidered bedspreads can be seen at the Ulster Museum.

ANNA ATKINS (1799–1871)

Anna Atkins, a woman of unusual intelligence, lived at a time when scientific discovery was moving at a tremendously exciting pace. Atkins managed to circumnavigate most of the restrictions imposed on her female contemporaries due to a tragedy. Her mother died within a year of her birth, so she was raised by her father, John George Children, who was clearly an emancipated man. Children was a scientist, mineralogist, and entomologist. He worked at the British Museum and saw no reason not to involve his daughter in his subjects, and Anna was fiercely interested in the things he taught her. A talented artist, she made accurate and beautiful watercolours and drawings of 256 shells to illustrate her father's translation of Jean Baptiste de Lamarck's catalogue *Genera of Shells* while still in her early twenties.

Anna was married to John Pelly Atkins in 1825, and after that we hear no more about him. They had no children, but we do know they went to live in the country, where Anna started to press the flowers and plants she found on her rambles through the Kentish countryside. Her beautifully annotated specimens were sent to botanists at Kew Gardens for research and the herbarium she made was donated to the British Museum in 1865.

In Kent she met Henry Fox Talbot, an inventor, scientist, and chemist generally attributed with inventing the calotype, a photographic process from which you could make prints. The daguerreotype was invented in France, literally a few weeks earlier, by Daguerre, who is generally considered the father of photography. In truth the two men were working on a very similar process at exactly the same time. Daguerre just got his patent first. Fox Talbot gave Anna a camera, though no work taken with it survives. More importantly, he shared with her the work he was doing with calotypes using paper coated with silver iodide, to which she turned her sharp and inquisitive mind.

Anna Atkins was fortunate to have access to many of her father's scientist friends. She was able to attend meetings at the Royal Society where new scientific innovations, such as nature printing, were being discussed by some of the greatest minds of the time. One of her father's friends was John Herschel, who invented the cyanotype photographic process in 1842. Cyanotype is a photographic printing process that involves exposing two chemicals, ferric ammonium citrate and potassium ferricyanide, to sunlight, creating a photographic record, or "blueprint," onto paper or cloth. Anna was fascinated by the process and quickly realized that placing pressed and dried plants with a strong structural shape directly onto the treated paper created a facsimile of a specimen that would be both scientifically interesting and ethereally beautiful.

She published her own work, *Photographs of British Algae: Cyanotype Impressions,* in 1843, which is considered to be the first book to be published using photographic images as illustrations, and which caused a great deal of interest in scientific circles. In 1853 she collaborated with her friend Anne Dixon to produce *Cyanotypes of British and Foreign Ferns* (John Paul Getty Museum), and in 1854, *Cyanotypes of British and Foreign Flowering Plants and Ferns*, which has been taken apart and is held in various museums and collections.

Very occasionally an original copy of *Photographs of British Algae: Cyanotype Impressions* comes onto the market. In 2004 a copy belonging to Robert Hunt sold for just shy of £250,000. Individual prints from *Cyanotypes of British and Foreign Flowering Plants and Ferns* made by Anne Dixon and Anna sell for thousands of dollars.

At our little yard in southeast London filled with artisans and artists, there are two artists who work with cyanotypes. One of them, Kasia Wozniak, collaborates with us. She has turned some of our plants and flowers into beautiful prints that we sell through our shop. I like to think Anna Atkins would be happy that the process continues today, less for the scientific research, but as a beautiful art form.

EMILY DICKINSON (1830–86)

Emily Dickinson was considered a pleasant, if eccentric, spinster from a good family in the small town of Amherst, Massachusetts, where she lived with her lawyer father and cold, unresponsive mother. Known today as one of America's best-loved poets, she saw only ten of her poems published during her lifetime.

What is less well known about Emily is that she was also an exceptional botanist. Long before she embarked on her writing, Emily made an herbarium of pressed flowers, which is remarkable for its delicacy and beauty. The collection is now housed at the Houghton Rare Book Library at Harvard University, where it is so fragile that even scholars are prohibited from studying it. Thankfully, it has been digitized and we are able to look at these tender pressings made by an intellectual and inquisitive young woman, who was hampered by the social mores of the times she lived in.

Each of the sixty-six pages of Emily's herbarium shows specimens exquisitely mounted and labelled in her spidery handwriting. Some plants are given their Latin or Linnaean names, and others their familiar names. They include the dates on which the specimens had been picked from the area around her home in Massachusetts. Although Emily's pressings were largely of native plants, she had a love for the exotic plants that had been naturalized in the area. The first page of her *Herbarium*, for example, is a study of the exotically scented jasmine. Her unexpected choice of jasmine for the first page of the herbarium could be considered symbolic of her hidden nature. Emily, a famous recluse, rarely glimpsed by her neighbours, invariably dressed in white

and was regarded as a puritanical and unworldly virgin obsessed by death and the fragility of life, was, in fact, a much more interesting and complicated person than her neighbours in Amherst could ever have imagined.

Her writings, published after her death, were carefully censored and it was not until a book of her letters, entitled *Open me carefully,* was published in 1998 that her passionate relationship with her friend, Susan Huntington, later to become her sister-in-law, showed a very different Emily. Despite her clear need for seclusion and privacy, Emily's letters to Susan show a vibrant, intellectual, scholarly mind with a lively interest in both family and village life. Far from being the distant, fragile hermit, her letters and poetry suggest a passionate and erotically charged woman, who almost certainly had a physical relationship with Susan Huntingdon, or, if she didn't, wished she had. It would be surprising if the poetry that touched and continues to affect so many was written by a woman who had no knowledge of love and the ways of the world.

Emily's herbarium and literary work are tangible signs of a woman who found an outlet for her creative and intellectual frustrations through the medium of poetry and pressing flowers.

ALICE EASTWOOD (1859–1953)

One of our favourite botanical heroines is Alice Eastwood. She was born in Toronto, Canada, but later moved to Denver in her teens, where she indulged her great love of nature, setting out into the countryside around her home with a press strapped to her back. Unlike many of her predecessors, Alice did go to school, where she was a star pupil, but her family's precarious financial situation meant she could not go on to university; instead, she took a job teaching high school. Her spare time was spent on her hobby, collecting flora to preserve and dissect. She became a familiar lone figure, hiking across wild terrains, with her shortened skirt for ease of mobility, sturdy boots, pony, and presses, pursuing an interest that was bordering on obsession, and for which she endured many hardships. She was robbed, lost, swept away by rivers, and camped out alone in brutal conditions while she waited for a specimen that she particularly wanted for her collection to bloom.

Alice was entirely self-taught, but she had no qualms about reaching out to leading botanists who were impressed with her knowledge and immaculately documented specimens. Eventually she came to the attention of eminent husband-and-wife botanists Kate and Townshend Brandegee, who hired her to help them with their herbarium, library, and extensive garden of native plants in San Diego. Together they made many trips, including to Baja, California, to add more species to their collection. Eventually amassing more than 75,000 specimens, the Brandegees donated their herbarium to the library at the University of California, where the three of them continued to work, collect, and catalogue plants.

The Brandegees, although keen botanists, were much less interested in the cataloguing of plants, but this was Alice's speciality. She designed a system of classification and special metal crates for the collection so it could be

89932
CALIFORNIA ACADEMY OF SCIENCES
FLORA OF CALIFORNIA
10341
Eschscholtzia
Santa Rosa
COLL. ALICE EASTWOOD
April 24, 1921

easily transported in case of a fire. Disaster struck with the 1906 San Francisco earthquake. Alice, having felt a tremor, considered it to be of no great concern and turned up to work as usual to find the surrounding buildings were on fire. Already the marble staircase in the Academy had collapsed. Hanging her lunch bag on the horn of some prehistoric exhibit and using the bronze banister for support, she slowly ascended hand over hand to the sixth floor and her beloved herbarium. The metal cases she had so carefully designed for just such an eventuality were useless in this situation. Quickly deciding which were the most important specimens to save, she bundled them up in sheets, which she lowered by rope to the ground floor. Appalled police and firefighters watched in terror as this seemingly mad lady risked her life to save some old dried-up plants. The 1,500 pressed plants she saved were rushed to safety, but the greater part of the collection was lost.

While California set about rebuilding the Academy, Alice travelled the United States and Europe, studying the great herbaria of the world, including the Gray Herbarium, the New York Botanical Garden, the National Museum of History in Paris, and the Royal Botanical Gardens at Kew. When the new building was completed in 1916, she returned to the Academy, which had been relocated to Golden Gate Park. For the rest of her long life, she painstakingly replaced all the lost species and included many more. By 1942 the collection stood at 333,000 species—three times the number of plants that had been destroyed in the fire. She continued to teach botany to the public, but more importantly she instructed the gardening staff of Golden Gate Park, helping it to become the renowned garden and arboretum it is today. She published more than 300 articles, was director of the San Francisco Botanical Club, and formed the American Fuchsia Society. At the age of ninety-one she travelled to Sweden, where she was made Honorary President of the International Botanical Congress and was seated in Linnaeus' chair. She died aged ninety-five, but her name lives on. Many of the plants she discovered were named after her and the Alice Eastwood Hall of Botany at the California Academy of Sciences, where you can still go and see botanical exhibitions, bears her name.

We love Alice Eastwood so much for her glorious courage and positivity, for the way she busted through that glass ceiling as if it wasn't there. After the earthquake and resulting fire that had destroyed her life's work up until that point, she said:

> I do not feel the loss to be mine, but it is a great loss to the scientific world and an irreparable loss to California. My own destroyed work I do not lament, for it was a joy to me while I did it, and I can still have the same joy in starting it again.

BEATRIX POTTER (1866–1943)

Beatrix Potter, a brilliant botanist and naturalist, cleverly circumvented the conventions and constrictions of her sex by turning her accurate illustrations of flora and fauna into whimsical children's tales. As a child she spent long hours at the Natural History Museum, a short walk from her London home, studying and sketching the insect collection. She was also inspired by *British Wild Flowers* by John E. Sowerby, a gift from her grandmother. Drawing and painting flowers was considered a perfectly ladylike pastime for young women, but Beatrix always combined her whimsical imagination with the empirical detachment of a scientist. I like to think that pressing flowers was almost certainly part of her process, in what she describes as the "careful botanical studies of my youth." Meticulous accuracy was her watchword, and the precision of her drawings of flora and fauna in her children's books probably goes a long way to explain how they have continued to be so successful for more than 150 years.

One of the worst examples of sexism at work in the nineteenth century was perpetrated against the twenty-year-old Beatrix Potter. The story about her meticulous study of mycology, accompanied by marvellous drawings of fungi, is maddening to read today. She went to great lengths to get an introduction to the foremost mycologist of that time, Charles Mackintosh. Under his guidance Beatrix studied the little-known subject of spore reproduction in fungi, lichens, and algae, writing a beautifully illustrated paper on her findings called "On the Germination of the Spores of Agaricineae." This scholarly work was then presented to the particularly misogynistic William Turner Thistelton-Dyer, who was director of Kew and president of the Linnean Society, and who described the work as "Mare's Nests."

Her ideas were rejected out of hand by the Society, who didn't even bother to look at the miraculous drawings she had made. Beatrix knew her studies were accurate, but accepted the slight with equanimity. A century later, the Linnaean Society issued an apology to Beatrix Potter and accepted that her work was, and still continues to be, of great importance. But Beatrix beat the system. Her children's stories went on to be so successful that she was able to gain her freedom; she left home and bought her own farm in the Lake District, becoming a passionate sheep farmer and buying the hill farms around her home as they came up for sale. Eventually she was custodian of 4,000 acres in the Lake District. When she died, she left the land to the National Trust, where it now forms a large part of the National Park and is home to two-thirds of the world's population of Herdwick sheep.

PRINCESS GRACE OF MONACO (1929–82)

One of the more unexpected flower pressers we discovered was Hitchcock's favourite actress, Academy Award-winning film star Grace Kelly, one of the most beautiful women to have ever graced the cinema screen (even perhaps, the Earth). In 1956, aged only twenty-six, she left Hollywood forever, leaving her family in Philadelphia to cross the seas and marry Prince Rainier of Monaco in a stunning ceremony. Just like a fairytale, Rainier took her away to live with him in a marvellous pink palace in the tiny principality where she remained, beautiful and enigmatic, locked away in her castle. She had three children—two beautiful but unruly daughters, and one son, HSH Prince Albert of Monaco, the present incumbent of the throne. Grace was one of the most famous women in the world, but from the moment she married, she never put a foot wrong, she remained the ice-cool princess, the epitome of decorum and restraint. Grace loved flowers, choosing for her wedding day a beautifully simple bouquet of lily of the valley. Over the years in Monaco, she began to press flowers from the palace gardens and turn them into pictures. Her pressed-flower works are rather touching in their pleasing "pristine formality"—not unlike the Princess herself. I like to think of her pressing flowers high up in her ivory tower, while the rich and carefree partied on the boats and in the casinos of her little kingdom. About pressing, she wrote in *My Book of Flowers*:

> Through working with flowers we began to discover things about ourselves that had been dormant. We found agility not only with our fingers but with our inner eyes in searching for line, scale and harmony. In bringing out these talents within ourselves, we gained a dimension that enabled us not only to search for harmony in an arrangement, but also to discover the importance of carrying it into our lives and our homes.

Two years later she tragically died when her car tumbled off a cliff road as she drove her daughter, Princess Stephanie, back to Monaco.

Guide

CYANOTYPE PRINTING

I discovered around the time of her last birthday that my nine-year-old niece, Renn, has a surprising fascination with Anna Atkins, the nineteenth-century botanist credited as the first female photographer, and first to publish a book illustrated with photographic images (see page 202). Renn learned about Anna's "sun-prints" at school, inspiring her to ask for an adorable illustrated book by Fiona Robinson titled *The Bluest of Blues—Anna Atkins and the First Book of Photographs* for her birthday. I was thrilled! I had a cyanotype kit in the studio that I'd been wanting to try out, so this was the perfect opportunity and would give Renn and I the chance to try the process together. We had already been working on a series of wildflower cyanotype prints for our online shop with photographer Kasia Wozniak, our studio neighbour who works with nineteenth-century photography techniques. We've since collaborated on a series of workshops where we do flower pressing in the morning, then head over to Kasia's studio in the afternoon to use pressed flowers to create cyanotype prints, which are always a great success.

After its invention in 1842, cyanotype printing was primarily used as a quick and cheap method of reproducing notes and diagrams, which is where the term "blueprints" comes from. It was a technique used by engineers to make copies of their drawings well into the twentieth century.

Anna Atkins, however, adapted cyanotype as a form of photography, encouraged by her friend Henry Fox Talbot, a pioneer of early photographs. She laid seaweed specimens directly onto paper coated with a solution of two chemicals—ferric ammonium citrate and potassium ferricyanide—to create a silhouette, then left the paper out in the sun to expose. The specimens would then be removed and the paper rinsed under cold running water to develop. The areas of the paper that were exposed to UV light turn blue, deepening in colour as the paper dries and leaving a ghost-like image of the object behind. The fascinating thing about Anna's cyanotypes, which were recorded in several books, is the amount of detail and depth that she managed to capture—some of the specimens look like three-dimensional objects photographed in their natural habitat, while others appear like X-rays. They are quite magical.

PROCESS

We recommend using a cyanotype kit for your first experiments, which will come with everything you need to get started, including detailed instructions. If you would like to do this with a child, make sure they wear gloves throughout and we would always advise the adult to mix and apply the chemical solution for them.

PAPER SELECTION

Most kits will come with paper, however, you might want to experiment with different paper finishes; for example, choose archival paper, which means it will be acid-free. This will help your prints to stand the test of time. Your paper also needs to stand up to being rinsed under the tap, so you don't want it to be too thin. Cartridge, watercolour, or cotton-rag paper all have slightly different qualities and are worth trying out. You can also print onto natural fabrics—cotton, linen, and silk all work well, but not synthetic fabrics.

TOOLS

We advise buying a complete cyanotype kit when you first try this, or your own kit should consist of:

Cyanotype emulsion in powder form—just add water
Glass contact frame with clips
Assorted papers with different textures
Sponge applicator brush
Measuring cup
Mixing cup
Disposable gloves
Clothes pegs
Flowers—we used wild vetch

1. Preparing your work area: If you're doing this on the kitchen table, cover it with newspaper before you begin and have something at the ready to mop up spillages. A plastic tray for developing your prints is useful if you can find one, and it is also good for collecting water drips when you hang up your print to dry.

2. Mix your solution and apply it to the paper: Put on your protective gloves. The chemical components come in powder form and will keep for many years; once mixed with water they will keep (separately) for up to a year, but once mixed together to make the solution, they will become light-sensitive immediately. You don't need to do this in complete darkness, but you do want to avoid exposing the solution to daylight at this stage, so working away from natural light is best. Add water to the two powders as per your kit instructions and shake well. Mix equal parts of the two chemicals together in a plastic cup using a wooden stirrer to make your solution. Apply an even layer to your paper using a sponge applicator and leave to dry in the dark. Make sure there isn't any pooling of the liquid on the paper.

3. Compose your flowers: Place your dried, coated paper onto a piece of board and lay your chosen flowers directly onto the paper. Pressed flowers work well for cyanotype prints as they lay flat against the paper to give you a strong silhouette. Choose flowers with interesting shapes, and experiment with flowers that have different qualities. A delicate poppy with its tissue-paper petals will give you a very different print than, say, a buck fern, which has a much more defined and solid leaf structure. Try fresh flowers, too, which will give more depth to your prints.

4. Lay glass over your composition and expose: Lay a sheet of glass over your composition and hold it into place with pegs or clips so the glass is pressing against the paper and holding your flowers in place. Set outside in direct sunlight and set a timer for 10 minutes. Angle your prints towards the sun, if you can.

5. Remove your flower and develop your print: Remove The glass and take away the flower. Place the paper in a plastic tray in the sink and rinse with cold running water. You will notice the colour of the paper changing immediately—the silhouette of the flower turns from a greeny yellow to the colour of the paper as the solution is washed away.

6. Hang up to dry: Once it has had a good rinse, hang your print up to dry and marvel at your creation!

My afternoon of printmaking with Renn was a great success. We picked dandelions, buttercups, vetch, and wild grasses from the fields close by and laid them all out on the dining table to make our compositions. Renn was in awe of the whole process, as was I. Barely half an hour after we'd picked the flowers we had our very own Anna Atkins-inspired prints using exactly the same process that she had almost 200 years earlier. I love the idea of little craft lessons like this inspiring children to become more aware of the nature around them. Hopefully in turn it will encourage them to think more about the fragile nature of our ecosystem and inspire them to take greater care of the planet, the future of which is ultimately in their little hands. And what a result that would be, coming from simple activities like this.

Story

TULIP

Nobody watched me before, now I am watched.
The tulips turn to me, and the window behind me
Where once a day the light slowly widens and slowly thins,
And I see myself, flat, ridiculous, a cut-paper shadow
Between the eye of the sun and the eyes of the tulips,
And I have no face, I have wanted to efface myself.
The vivid tulips eat my oxygen.
"Tulips," Sylvia Plath (1932–63)

The tulip is, to me, the most human of all the cut flowers. In Sylvia Plath's poem "Tulips," these flowers have become the enemy. In this extract the very qualities about it that we love have become threatening to Plath in her fragile mental state and heightened awareness. The tulips seem to be watching her, stealing the air she breathes.

Tulips are unruly. They not only continue to grow in the vase long after they have been cut, but they also react to temperature and light. How many times have you left your tulips standing up like soldiers, to come down the next morning and find them wide open, sprawled across the table, hanging out of the vase, looking, for all the world, as if they have had a night out on the tiles? Cut them again and refresh the water with an ice cube and a few hours later they will be standing straight again, looking only a little the worse for wear from the exuberances of the night before.

A fellow florist, Flora Starkey, made an enchanting timelapse video of tulips (which you can see on her website, www.florastarkey.com). She arranged them in vases and left them to get on with just being tulips. In the film we can see the tulips literally dancing, but what struck me most was that they weren't all moving in the same direction. Each flower seemed to have a life of its own, twisting and turning, bowing and straightening up. It's one of the most joyous and beautiful things I have ever seen.

Tulips have a fascinating history, which has been the subject of many books. Here it is in brief, but if you want to know more, some recommendations include Anna Pavord's *The Tulip*, Deborah Moggach's *Tulip Fever*, and Alexandre Dumas' *The Black Tulip*. In 1562, an Ottoman cloth merchant sent a gift of tulip bulbs to his counterpart in Antwerp, who, imagining they were an exotic sort of onion, roasted and ate most of them. Possibly because they didn't taste very nice, he planted the few remaining bulbs in his garden. The following spring the first tulips grown in Europe appeared.

To this day, tulips are considered to be more Dutch than clogs or round wax-covered cheeses, more Amsterdam than legal marijuana, coffee houses, or hookers in brightly lit windows. But in fact the tulip originated centuries ago in the foothills of the Tien Shen mountains on the Chinese–Russian–Afghan borders. From there they made their way, via the Silk Road, to Turkey and Persia, where they were taken up by the Ottoman Empire as a symbol of their wealth, culture, and power. Tulips were grown in every Imperial garden. They made frequent appearances in the poetry of Rumi, Omar Khayyam, and Hafiz. Their beautiful scarlet flowers adorn iznik tiles, the brocaded robes of Sultan Suleiman, Levni miniatures, carpets, and embroidery.

The first botanist to bring tulip bulbs to Europe was Carolus Clusius, possibly as a result of seeing the tulips in the garden of the hapless cloth merchant. The flower was soon taken up by the Dutch with the same enthusiasm as it had been by the Ottomans.

The tulip came to symbolize wealth, style, and status in Holland, and people began to collect the bulbs, even resorting to stealing them from the gardens of the wealthy. Giant tulipieres were created by the great porcelain makers of Delft to show off each marvellous flower individually. Artists like Ambrosius Bosschaert the Elder were commissioned to paint the tulip in exquisite artworks, featuring two of the most precious and coveted bulbs: "Semper Augustus," white with red striation; and "Viceroy," yellow with red flairs. The appearance of exotic tulips in the great Dutch flower paintings only added to their fame and reputation.

Over four years during the Dutch Golden Age, between 1633 and 1637—a time that was later known as "tulipomania"—tulip bulbs became so valued that their price skyrocketed. A single tulip bulb exchanged hands for the same price as a house in the most exclusive part of Amsterdam, or six times the average person's annual salary. Then suddenly, as fast as the bubble had blown up, it burst and the market crashed. Many people were left holding bulbs in which they had invested their entire savings, now worth no more than the single flower that would bloom and die. The tulip flower was unlikely to perform as well, if at all, the second year round. Today, tulipomania is still taught to young financiers as the first example of a market bubble and crash.

A sad irony is that the most beautiful and desired tulips of all, the "broken" tulip, *Tulipa* "Semper Augustus," with its coloured flares on a white background, is actually the result of a virus that was weakening the plant, so as it delighted the eye, the plant was dying. The "Semper Augustus" species is now extinct and, despite all the skills of botanists and breeders, nobody has ever managed to reproduce its original exquisite form. Broken tulips were highly unpredictable, often appearing in completely unexpected colours, or reverting to plain white, but when they performed it was something to behold, entrancing artists and taste-makers alike, but all the while the precious bulb was doomed.

Clusius wrote in 1585, "…any tulip thus changing its original colour is usually ruined afterwards and so wanted only to delight its master's eyes with this variety of colours before dying, as if to bid him a last farewell." Reading

this I was struck how Clusius, like Plath, has also given the tulip an almost human status, attributing emotion and endeavour to the flower.

The dancing tulip in its myriad forms and colours has held us spellbound through the centuries. It is just a flower, but it has inspired great art, poetry, and literature. It has driven people to madness and even suicide, it has made and destroyed fortunes. Today people flock to the tulip fields in April to see the vast acres striped like a Bridget Riley painting.

Many attempts have been made to press tulips, mostly resulting in mouldy messes. The tulip has a strong filament and juicy stem that are difficult to press, often rotting before they dry. However, we have had some good successes amid the many failures. Second-year tulips that have become weakened and are less fleshy often make the best pressings. Otherwise we have taken to dissecting the tulip, pressing the stem, the filament, and the stamens separately from the petals, then reconstructing them in the final piece. We have also attempted to remove the moisture very quickly in the microwave before laying the tulip between the pages of the press to finish the drying and flattening process. Sometimes we wonder, do they even want to be pressed?

Story

JASMINE

In the pretty cobbled yard outside our studio, there is a magnificent jasmine plant. It is very mature and climbs the wall of the lute makers'. Twice, sometimes three times a year, it flowers, filling the air with fragrance. The more we cut it, the more shoots appear, coiling and twisting round each other, as they fight through their own thatch to reach for the sun. Nobody except us prunes the plant and one year half of it crashed off the wall, dragging some festoon lights and electric wires with it. But it quickly bounced back. We cut long, curly trails when it is in bud, or even just for the leaf, and press them. Jasmine is the perfect elegant border plant for using in mixed pieces.

Tamil Nadu: January. We had left grey, damp England and woken up at a peculiar time to a dusty Indian dawn. We walked out along a jungly road towards the village, the sun appearing like a 20-watt bulb, dimly yellow, rising through the mist. We walked past three little palm shacks where an elderly woman was making chai over a small fire. From one of these unpromising houses two girls appeared, immaculate in jade and peacock

saris, their hair long and glossy with coconut oil. One had an enviably thick plait, the other had her hair loose. Each girl's hair was beautifully adorned with fresh jasmine flowers. Around their ankles more flowers were strung together. The perfume of jasmine and coconut reached us on the warm breeze. We were grey with lack of sleep and sunshine, and scruffy in clothes creased from the suitcase; I remember feeling ungainly and ashamed. These girls had so little but they came out of their modest home as beautifully turned out as any model on a catwalk. I doubt I have ever looked as fresh and lovely and considered as they did that early morning in Tamil Nadu.

Another particularly engaging image that springs to mind is Jane Birkin standing in front of the pyramids, gazing dreamily at the giant sphinx with ropes of jasmine round her neck in the 1978 film of *Death on the Nile*.

The jasmine flower is so ancient and deeply rooted in Asian culture that nobody can say for certain where it originated. In *The Garden Flowers of China*, written in the third century CE, *Jasmine officinale* and *Jasminum sambac* are recorded as foreign plants. The name jasmine comes from the Persian, meaning "Gift of God" and it is likely that the flower originated somewhere in Central Asia. The Chinese name *Yeh Hsi Minh* is a corruption of the Persian name. *Jasmine officinale* and *Jasminum sambac* likely arrived in Europe via Sicily with the Arab invasions in 827 CE, but there is no definite proof of this. Indeed, until Bocaccio's *Decameron* in the fourteenth century, there are no European texts describing jasmine, so nobody really knows when it came to Europe, but it is so obliging and easy to grow that it has become ubiquitous, growing in every part of the world except the North and South Poles. Jasmine is an essential part of the culture of Central and Southeast Asia. We know that Jasmine has been growing in the UK since at least 1548, when it is mentioned in William Turner's *Names of Herbes*. By the time Carl Linnaeus came to name it, it had become so thoroughly naturalized in Europe that he thought it was a native plant of Switzerland.

Jasmine represents beauty and sensuality, it is said to be both an aphrodisiac and anti-depressant, as well as an aid to sleep. Certainly, to plant a jasmine near a bedroom window or at the entrance to your house is to fill your guest with a sense of welcome, pleasure, and wellbeing. In religious ceremonies, jasmine represents purity and wisdom.

Many Hindu temples are decorated with depictions of the *Madurai Malligai* jasmine flower, and certainly no wedding is complete without garlands and leis of jasmine flowers around the necks, wrists, ears, and ankles of the deities, and also of the bride and groom. Many flowers with such a strong scent annoy people, but there is something so subtle and poignant about this flower's fragrance that it causes little offence, only pleasure.

Jasmine is unsurprisingly the base of many fragrances, with an intensity and musky tone beneath sweet floral top notes. An oily extraction from macerated flower heads has been used to perfume the hands and throats of ladies for centuries. Initially the process known as enfleurage was done by pressing flowers into animal fat, which then took on the scent of the flower before being extracted after the flowers had done their work. These days the process is more sophisticated, but nevertheless it takes hundreds of thousands of flower heads to produce a few millilitres of the "absolute," the base oil from which perfumes are constructed. It is extremely expensive to produce, but is one of the most valued ingredients in the world of perfume, where it is known simply as "La Fleur"—apart from the rose, there is no other flower so highly prized by the "noses," who are the people with magnificent olfactory skill who create fragrance for the great houses of fashion and perfume.

Known simply as The Lady, Burma's (Myanmar's) Aung San Suu Kyi was probably the world's most renowned and courageous prisoner of conscience. A delicate beauty, tempered with steel, she never appeared in public without flowers in her hair, usually orchids and jasmine. Aung San Suu Kyi was under house arrest in Rangoon for fifteen years, separated from her English husband and two sons. Her dignified, defiant resistance in the face of oppression won her the Nobel Peace Prize in 1991. Jasmine came to symbolize all she stood for. Her beautiful appearance and hair dressed with the fragrant flowers became a beacon for justice and democracy. Aung San Suu Kyi's powerful stance caught the attention of the world and plaques celebrating her were erected in many cities, usually accompanied by a jasmine plant. When she was finally released she learned that her granddaughter had been born in England. The baby was named Jasmine. I wish I could end the story here, but unfortunately, since she gained her freedom in 2015 and became leader of Myanmar, her perfect record has been besmirched due to her ignoring the violence against the Rohingya Muslims in her country.

Wandering home after dinner up an unmade track somewhere near the Po de Leo, in Ibiza, we became aware of little cairns of stacked stones, and then of the man who made them. He seemed to be the hippie who went for a party in the 1960s and stayed on. He muttered at us and his dog barked, terrifying the children. We ran the last part of the way to the house, where we caught it, wafting through the air, the most exquisite fragrance. That was the first time. Sometimes called *Delice de Noche* (sweetness of the night) or *Dama de Noce* (lady of the night), it is also known as night-scented jasmine. I shouldn't really include it here as it is not a true jasmine, but part of the olive family. Night-scented jasmine, or *Cestrum nocturnum*, is from the Solanaceae, or potato family, like deadly nightshade. You walk past it in the day without a second glance. The shrub looks dull when the tubular flowers are closed and there is no fragrance, but as dusk falls the flowers open to release their intoxicating scent. Although probably discovered by Christopher Columbus in the West Indies, this jasmine is now found in sub-tropical and temperate, frost-free climates around the world.

In the world of perfume, apart from the rose, there is no other flower so highly prized by the "noses."

The Philippinos have a story of a young sultan, Datu, who took a poor but extraordinarily beautiful girl called Dama to be his bride. She was unable to have a child, so the sultan grew angry and treated her unkindly, refusing to eat the wonderful meals she prepared for him, or admire the exquisite flowers she arranged, and soon began returning home late, or not at all. Dama was sad and couldn't eat or sleep, then became ill. When Datu eventually came home he found his wife was dying. She did not reproach him, but smiled and told him how much she loved him. After she died he missed her unbearably and remembered what a wonderful wife she had been. He and the village mourned together and one day he visited her grave and found a new shrub growing there. He tended the plant lovingly and one night he was rewarded with a sweet perfume, the cut stems filling the house with fragrance again as it had when Dama was alive. When many years later the Spaniards arrived in the Philippines, they too noticed the delicious perfume and were told the sad story of Dama. So they named the flower *Dama de Noche* and took cuttings home and, as legend has it, that is how night-scented jasmine arrived in Europe. It is the national flower of the Philippines where the flowers of *Jasminum sambac* are strung into leis, corsages, and crowns.

Jasmine is one of the most evocative flowers. Scent, as we know, is the strongest of the senses for creating memory and it is strongly linked with romance and religion. We love to press jasmine when it is in bud, but not so much once it is in flower, as the white flowers tend to turn brown. There are some pretty pink (*beesianum*) and yellow (*officinale*) varieties that are excellent for pressing; not to be confused with winter jasmine or forsythia, which is a false jasmine and hopeless for pressing, as is the architect's favourite, *Trachelospermum jasminoides*, an evergreen variety that produces flowers of exquisite fragrance in mid- to late summer.

Project

SKETCH MAYFAIR WINDOWS

In May 2019, we were invited back to Sketch in London's Mayfair to design an installation for their annual Mayfair Flower Show, and were asked to respond to a loose theme of "Arts and Crafts." We enjoy working to a brief, it encourages us to thread a narrative through the work we create. We are endlessly inspired by the process of visual research, drawing on historical references and imagery to develop our story and inform our decisions.

Our response to this particular brief was inspired by the stained-glass windows designed by Edward Burne-Jones for William Morris' Red House in Bexleyheath, Kent, in 1859. The house was co-designed by Morris with the architect Philip Webb, not only as a family home, but also as the collaborative hub of his artistic community. Heavily influenced by Morris' ethos of craftsmanship and artisan skills, it remains an excellent early example of what later became known as the Arts and Crafts movement. The movement began in England in the 1860s, when artists rebelled against the social norms of Victorian England in an attempt to reform design and decoration in Britain, standards of which the movement's leader, Morris, believed had rapidly declined as a result of mechanised factory production brought about by the Industrial Revolution.

Everything inside the house was designed by William Morris and his friends, from the furniture, wallpaper, and fabrics to wallhangings and stained-glass windows. The pleasure that this collective of artists and designers took from working together on Red House led to the formation of Morris & Co. in 1875, a design guild that set out to produce furnishings and decorative arts for the home that united beauty, craftsmanship, and utility.

What we love about the stained glass in particular is the simplicity and playful design of the floral forms. The first wallpaper pattern to be issued by Morris & Co. was "Daisy," a simple design of meadow flowers said to be directly influenced by late medieval "mille-fleurs" tapestries and sixteenth-century woodcuts from the "herbals" of the time. Similar daisies can be seen in the stained glass at Red House, painted bright orange and yellow with dainty stems and delicate, feathery leaves. They are simple and stylized, but perfect little specimens that look as if they could have been pressed inside the glass.

As we began to develop our idea for this project, we came across a series of images taken at Château Astremoine, an abandoned chateau in northern France. In particular, an enchanting photograph of a brightly coloured, floral stained-glass window. The window is designed as though looking out over an overgrown garden, with painted grape vines up above and traces of

honeysuckle trailing down through each pane of glass. At the bottom of the frame, blue bearded iris, coral peonies, and bright pink garden roses grow up from the ground, appearing to be pressing against the glass from the outside. It's an image we go back to again and again for inspiration. The design was in stark contrast to the perfection we saw at Red House, but we loved how the flowers appear to be growing naturally through the framework of the windows.

The idea of the Victorian glasshouse, left abandoned for nature to take over, alongside the romantic ideals and decorative features of the Arts and Crafts movement were rich sources of inspiration for this project. Our idea was to create an indoor garden based on an overgrown Victorian conservatory, using pressed British garden flowers to create an interpretation of these beautiful stained-glass windows.

The space we were allocated at Sketch was quite a challenge—a large corner of the reception area with an enormous, immovable artwork on the main wall that had to be covered, then a wide staircase going down to the restaurant with an equally huge display cabinet that also needed to be hidden, not moved. This meant we had to design a freestanding set to wrap around the space and support our windows.

We designed a framework for four large arched windows, three of which would sit side by side on the long wall, and one would stand alone. For the three together, we wanted them to have a similar feel to the abandoned chateau, with flowers growing through the frame, as if growing naturally in the garden. The stand-alone window would be different, each pane would have a single species of flower within it, with detailing in the corners, echoing the design of the windows at Red House. A smaller square window would sit inside another freestanding frame built to wrap around the cabinet at the bottom of the stairs that was made entirely of pressed ferns—an homage to the Victorian fern hunters (see page 88).

Using glass was going to be too risky in terms of breakage and the weight of the material, both in the studio and during installation. Instead, we had samples of Perspex sent to the studio for testing. We wanted the windows to be lit from behind with diffused light. After several experiments with smaller pieces, we found the best solution was to use a sheet of frosted Perspex at the back, onto which the flowers were laid, then a clear sheet on top to allow the flowers to be highly visible. As soon as we started to experiment, we found the use of light completely enhanced the flowers' beauty. Every tiny detail came into sharp focus—the veins running through their leaves, the patterns

on their petals. Folds, creases, and layers accentuated subtle differences in tone and colour.

Ten enormous sheets of Perspex arrived at the studio, each one 2 metres (6.5 feet) in height and a hell of a lot heavier than we expected, so getting them up and down the narrow, rickety staircase of our studio was a challenge. Eventually we worked out that they could be levered up through the double doors of our first-floor Victorian studio that slide wide-open onto the yard, but this was a feat in itself.

To plot out the design for the arches and the spacing of the window panes, we used big rolls of tracing paper to create templates that were placed underneath the Perspex to mark out the curve of the arch and the grid for the panes. The spacing was very important for the design and we thought of a simple trick to make each window feel more authentic, sourcing self-adhesive lead strip tape to create the illusion of individual panes.

The designs for each of the windows evolved naturally as we delved into our archive of pressings. We wanted to use as many jewel-bright colours as we could to make the pieces sing. To get the feel of a garden, we layered the flowers, starting with taller-stemmed feature flowers—butterfly ranunculus, opium, and field poppies—which all hold their colour well. Clematis, snake's head fritillaries, lisianthus, and cosmos snipped from Melissa's garden had dainty stems, which were essential to keep the focus on the shapes and colours of the flower heads, rather than the stems having to fight for space. At the very bottom we placed tiny violas, as if creeping up from the flower bed, adding ferns and rose leaves for a punch of green, and to hide blunt or bare stems. In the central window we placed our prized possession, a red-and-yellow-striped parrot tulip—the very best of our tulip-pressing experiments. At the time of making this piece, our tulip pressings had been fairly disastrous, so this beauty took pride of place.

Long-stemmed sweet peas on the vine and dicentra (bleeding hearts) creeping in from the outer edges helped to connect it all together. We left space in the centre of the outer windows, trying not to overcrowd the overall design. To tackle the empty space in the arched area, we placed trails of jasmine we'd collected from just outside our studio and we were pleased with how it drifted around elegantly.

Settling on the final designs seemed to happen naturally as we fiddled with the layout to achieve the right balance of shape and colour. Once we were happy with the positioning, we took photographs for reference before each of the flowers were glued into place one by one. Once we had a few flowers in place, they were weighed down with heavy books to dry, before adding more stems in layers. Each window took around a day and a half to glue into place once the design was settled.

Once dry, the clear-Perspex layer was placed over the final design and the two layers were simply taped together at the edges for ease. This was a cheap and quick solution as the edges would be hidden by a wooden frame for the installation. We then taped the rolls of sticky lead window strip onto the top of the Perspex, carefully following the template to create the window panes.

We found that the two pieces of Perspex bulged quite considerably in the middle, creating a gap between the layers, so taping them together tightly was quite a challenge. It was too late to try to resolve the issue, but we did find a solution for the future, in drilling holes and riveting the layers together with clear Perspex screws and bolts.

The build for this job was complicated due to the scale and awkwardness of the space at Sketch. Noise restrictions after a certain time meant that if we didn't get it loaded in, constructed, and completed in one go, we had to down tools, take it all down and come back the following night to start again. I say this speaking from experience, as this is exactly what happened.

The set had been built offsite to our specifications. Each section was heavy and clunky and had to be loaded in piece by piece. The windows had to be laid into the frames and fixed into position with wooden batons and great precision. Installing in a listed building also presented its own set of issues. There were just too many obstacles to overcome in one night. After a lot of begging and pleading with the crew, and a couple of last-minute call-ins, we managed to pull together a team for a second overnight install and got the

job done with a couple of hours left to style the space with trailing ivy, tropical plants, ferns, and our favourite Victorian daybed from the studio.

All the while, we managed to keep our weekly contracts and daily flower deliveries going, as well as major installations at the Chelsea Flower Show, a wedding in France, and some sculptures for Badminton House, while also trying to make time to put the final arrangements together for my own wedding—the grand finale of a phenomenally busy summer. Eventually, off we trundled to North Wales, where I finally got to throw my own flower-filled party.

Towards the end of all of this madness, on Midsummer's Eve, our pressed-flower windows went to the V&A to form the backdrop to a Preen by Thornton Bregazzi fashion show. Preen was founded in 1996, built on an aesthetic of Arts and Crafts-inspired florals and modern graphic lines. For the show, the designers showcased pieces celebrating the summer solstice, themed around natural floral motifs and pagan references. We were delighted for the windows to have another trip out to the V&A, the dream venue for this collaboration.

Story

SWEET PEA

Here are sweet peas, on tip-toe for a flight:
With wings of gentle flush o'er delicate white,
And taper fingers catching at all things,
To bind them all about with tiny rings.
"I Stood Tiptoe Upon a Little Hill," John Keats (1795–1821)

When I was a child, sweet peas were grown in the vegetable garden for cutting. Teepees of hazel sticks were tied with brown string, which smelled of tar, to provide a frame for the elegant little flower to scramble up. The plants spent long months in the greenhouse getting strong roots, being regularly pinched out to make them stronger. Finally, when they were about 5cm (2 inches) high, they were planted out when the ground was still cold and wintry. By May we had our reward and masses of multicoloured flowers thronged the teepees. Sweet peas love to be trimmed regularly; the more you cut, the more you get. Once cut and in vases, the whole house would fill up with their delicious fragrance.

Sweet peas, especially on the vine with their curly tendrils, make the most beautiful pressed flowers. We cut long swathes and place them in large presses to get the tentacles, tendrils, and buds into the finished piece.

Lathyrus odoratus literally means sweet-scented pea. Above all others, the sweet pea has the most delicious scent and beautiful, arching blooms, swift in the vase, but constantly producing new flowers, so that one good pot of sweet peas can keep you in flowers (and pressings) all summer long. That seems to be all that is necessary for its existence.

The first sweet pea arrived in England when Father Francisco Cupani, a seventeenth-century Franciscan monk and renowned naturalist and botanist, sent some seeds of a fragrant bi-coloured wild pea from Sicily to Dr Robert Uvedale, a keen collector of rare and unusual plants. At the same time he also sent seeds to Dr Caspar Commelin in Amsterdam, who published an article on sweet peas in 1701, including the first botanical drawing of the flower. I love to think of this clever, gentle monk collecting seeds under clear, blue skies in the beautiful Mediterranean island of Sicily and sending them out into the world. He essentially gifted us with one of our best-loved flowers. You can still buy the same wild sweet pea named after Cupani; it is the most fragrant of them all. My mother-in-law has a Cupani sweet pea that returns every year, scrambling through the untidy paving stones outside her ancient cottage in Buckinghamshire. Last year I made loads of pressings from her patch. When pressed, the Cupani peas come out quite a bright blue and are especially delicate and translucent. The colour fades quite quickly, but the form remains perfect.

Almost 100 years after Father Cupani dispatched his seeds, a Scottish horticulturalist called Henry Eckford started to manipulate the breeding of the plant in Wem, in Shropshire, developing the wild and fragile little climber from Sicily into the queen of annuals. The sweet pea "Grandiflora" varieties that we know and love today were the result of this "prince of specialists" work (to quote Liberty Hyde Bailey). In 1901 Silas Cole, a keen fan of Eckford and his peas, who was head gardener to Earl Spencer, was fortunate enough to find a natural mutation in his garden that he named The Countess Spencer, after the wife of his boss (incidentally, an ancestor of Princess Diana). This sweet pea had frilly edges and a long wing, as well as the long stems that make it so good for cutting. Descendants of this species can still be found today.

The Victorians adored the sweet pea. It was a completely new flower to them, relatively easy to grow with its magnificent profusion of pretty, candy coloured flowers and delicate, haunting scent. They loved to give meanings to flowers, so apparently sweet peas are associated with departures and goodbyes. I don't know why, maybe because of the scent that lingers after the beloved has already departed.

> The Victorians adored the sweet pea, with its magnificent profusion of pretty, candy coloured flowers and delicate, haunting scent.

I have a perennial sweet pea *Lathyrus latifolius* that returns every year and is one of my favourite things in the whole garden. It was there when we bought the house thirty years ago and returns every May without fail. There is a white one and several bright pink ones whose flowers fade to blue and lavender before setting seed. As long as I keep cutting the flowers before the pea pods fatten, it just keeps on flowering until early October. But it doesn't have a scent; it isn't really a sweet pea, just a flowering scentless pea. But nonetheless, it makes excellent pressings.

Today there are more than 100 varieties of sweet pea and almost as many obsessed specialists endlessly creating yet more species. You have only to visit Chelsea Flower Show and see and smell the magnificent displays; it's like being in a sweet shop. There are frilly ones and fancy ones, striped, rippled, and marbled ones, picotee with their petals tipped in a different colour, almost-black ones through myriad colours, and shades of pinks and purples to purest white. This flower has few faults, the seeds are poisonous if eaten, so don't do that, and, in my experience, they are heavy drinkers and need a lot of water; they are also prone to powdery mildew and dislike being grown on the same patch of earth for too many years in a row. If you decide to grow them, take the advice freely available to you online. If you don't, it is quite easy to go wrong, but if you get it right, you can have a pot full of deliciously scented blooms in your cutting garden or scrambling over your patio or sunny balcony in return for a tiny investment.

Project & Guide

PRESSED FLOWER WINDOWS

Just a stone's throw from Melissa's home in South London is one of our favourite private gardens, owned by Daisy Garnet, our dear friend and collaborator on many of our more ambitious planting projects. It is always a treat to pay a visit to the garden, a place Talena, JamJar Flowers' Head Florist, and I now frequent for our weekly gardening fix.

Talena and I both changed careers from fashion to floristry at a similar time and went straight into working with cut flowers at JamJar, with very little knowledge of growing or caring for plants in the garden. The more we work with seasonal flowers, especially the beautiful British varieties we are seeing more and more from local growers, the more we want to get our own hands into the earth to better understand the cycles of nature and the plants and flowers that we work with and adore. Daisy kindly took us under her wing one cold and frosty February afternoon and has been sharing her gardening wisdom ever since, while we help to weed, water, sow, and snip. Her allotment plot has become our little sanctuary where we can switch off and get back to basics.

One very hot August afternoon, Melissa and I took an archive box of pressed flowers over to Daisy's garden to try out a new idea. Light floods into the house through Georgian windows, offering the perfect framework for a pressed-flower window piece. With Daisy elbow-deep in the mulberry tree at the end of the garden, her arms blood red with its juice, we sheltered from the heat under the grape vine and started to lay out our pressed specimens.

Having created pressed-flower windows for Sketch a few years back—arranging pressed stems between two sheets of Perspex—we wondered if we could achieve something similar using simple everyday materials that we had to hand. By creating a pressed-flower piece in an exterior window we'd be purposefully exposing the specimens to direct sunlight, so the vibrant colour in some flower specimens would inevitably fade quickly. We wanted to create this piece with flowers that had already faded, or had little colour to begin with, to minimize the change in colour over time. We chose to use jasmine, sweet peas, and dicentra to echo some of the shapes and textures that can be found growing in the garden.

We often find jasmine to be a useful specimen when creating a larger-scale piece, especially for evoking a sense of movement within the frame. A scrambler by nature, its long, wiry stem twists and turns as it grows. With very little love and attention it will grow in abundance, however, just one or two pressed stems can really elevate a design. When pressed, its organic shape is easily retained, resulting in an elegant silhouette. A delicate tracery of pressed jasmine gives a sensation of the flowers growing behind or through the window panes.

Sweet peas produce tiny clasping tendrils to help them climb and grow, as they reach out in search of support. When placed in front of diffused light, I love how their petals look like an X-ray, the folds creating shadow and depth in subtle tones of creamy beige through to dusky pink. An excellent flower for pressing, and perfect for this type of project. Lastly, we added two or three stems of dicentra, or "bleeding heart," its adorable heart-shaped flowers hanging from slender, arching stems offer elegant detailing as they string out into the frame.

We made this piece as an experiment, so for ease we opted for simple strips of masking tape to attach each stem to good-quality tracing-paper panels, which we'd cut to size to fit each window pane. The paper pieces were simply taped to the back of the window as a temporary measure. On seeing this piece come together, we were pleased with the aesthetic nature of the tape, a nod to the long-established method of mounting specimens with this material for botanical study, a simple detail present in the many thousands of herbarium collections across the globe.

We can imagine this as a beautiful window treatment for privacy in a bathroom or a ground-floor window looking directly onto the street. You could either use these simple materials or make a more permanent piece by replacing the window pane with two sheets of glass—one frosted and one clear—with the pressed flowers secured between them.

TOOLS

Tracing paper
Pencil
Box cutter and cutting board
Metal ruler
Masking tape
Scissors
Pressings: we used jasmine, sweet peas, dicentra

1. Choose an appropriate window—a fan light or an internal door with glass panes would be perfect.

2. Hold your tracing paper up against the glass and mark the corners with a pencil. Cut to size using a box cutter and metal ruler for precision. Tape your tracing-paper pieces to a board or a flat surface.

3. Lay out your flowers, starting with your largest specimen. Choose stems with an interesting silhouette. We placed jasmine first, starting at the top, snipping the stems to fit to size, encouraging the line of the stem to follow through to the next panel.

4. Play around with the composition, placing sweet peas and dicentra creeping in from the edges of the frame. Think about how the flowers would grow naturally when placing them. Take care not to over fill, often negative space is just as important for the composition to feel balanced.

5. When you are happy with your placement, secure each stem into position with thin strips of masking tape and trim any overhanging stems.

TIP: Using a knife or sharp scissors, make several score marks across the roll of masking tape in horizontal lines around 3mm thick. This will allow you to peel off small strips to tape down your flowers, rather than trying to cut each strip at the same thickness with scissors.

6. Secure the tracing paper onto the back of your window using masking tape, or use double-sided tape along the edges.

Story

DAISY

To see this flower agenst the sunne spread,
whan it upriseth early by the morrow,
that blissful sight softeneth all my sorrow.
"The Legend of Good Women," Geoffrey Chaucer (1342/43–1400)

Did you make daisy chains when you were a child? Slitting the stems with a sharp fingernail and threading the stem of another daisy through the opening you had made? Later, did you sit in the star-studded grass and pull the petals off one by one? He loves me…he loves me not…he loves me. The object of your devotion would probably be playing cricket miles away, bowling a low fast ball known as a "daisy cutter," without an inkling that somewhere a girl was shredding daisies and trying to create magic to make him love her. This is not a new phenomenon. Goethe has the pregnant Margherita pulling petals off daisies to try to work out how Faust felt about her.

There are over 32,000 plants in the Asteraceae family, which is second only to orchids in the vast number of species that range from the smallest *Bellis perennis* daisy to the sunflower. Today we are concentrating on the white daisies with yellow centres that grow wild and wanton on our lawns, in our hedgerows, and between the cracks in the paving stones. Even with this distinction, there are still very many varieties.

In Anglo Saxon they are called *dæges eage*, or "day's eye," because they open their eyes all day and close them at night like an innocent, obedient child who will awake from a dreamless sleep "fresh as a daisy." According to Celtic myth, when children died the gods scattered daisies to honour them, and daisies planted with primroses set in moss are a symbol of a mother's love.

In Latin, the garden daisy's name is *Bellis perennis*, meaning, possibly and simply, perennial beauty. But *Bellis* may mean other things, too. We know that Linnaeus drew many of his flower names from the ancient myths, and there is a story where a nymph called Belides turned herself into a daisy to avoid the unwanted attentions of the lusty Vertumnus, the Etruscan god of gardens, agriculture, and seasons. So Bellis may be a corruption of Belides. Another theory is that the name has its roots in the Latin word for war, "*bellum*," from which we get the word "bellicose." When the Romans went to war they took sackfuls of daisy heads with them, as the juice extracted from them was believed to help with the healing of wounds. Indeed, some of the old names for daisy are bruisewort and woundwort, because bandages were soaked in the pressings of daisies to help soothe and heal a wound. In Scotland the daisy is sometimes called bairnwort, a nod to the way it has always fascinated little children, and another proclamation of it being symbolic of innocence.

There are ox-eye daisies (*Leucanthemum vulgare*), also called dog daisies, which are the ones you see growing wild in meadows and on verges beside roads all over Europe, Asia, North America, New Zealand, and Australia. Then there is feverfew (*Tanacetum parthenium*) with its multi-flowered heads and fragrant leaves that are a cure for migraines—these will grow like a weed in your gravel garden if you give them half a chance.

From the Canary Islands come marguerite or Paris daisy (*Argyranthemum frutescens*), which have a greyish leaf and are often trained into little standards and used for ornamental gardens. Then there is chamomile, the most efficacious of them all (*Matricaria chamomilla* and *Matricaria nobile*), which looks very similar to the ox-eye daisy but has a different leaf structure. Chamomile tea, the most soothing and fragrant drink, supposedly alleviates anxiety and aids restful sleep.

After being chased by Mr McGregor, the extremely frightened Peter Rabbit in Beatrix Potter's children's stories is fed chamomile tea by his worried mother. I hope she had a cup herself.

I am a big fan of Mary Wesley, who had her first novel, evocatively entitled *The Camomile Lawn*, published at the age of seventy. A chamomile lawn is really a sort of daisy meadow and I have always longed for one—to spend an afternoon sleeping in its fragrance seems the very height of decadent pleasure. Chamomile, both flower and leaf, is an ingredient in many craft beers and soothing medicines.

Easy to grow and hard to kill, daisies have been delighting people since Roman times and for centuries before; there is evidence of them being used as decoration on 4,000-year-old Egyptian pottery, and daisies decorating hair clips found in Crete date back to the Minoan culture. So many affectionate phrases attach themselves to daisies, including "Oops a daisy" for a little fall. "Pushing up the daisies" is a light-hearted way of describing death. It's a favourite name, along with buttercup for a cow, but while buttercups are toxic to cows, daisies supposedly relax the animal and increase milk yield. It is a diminutive pet name of Margaret or Marguerite, although nowadays people just call their little girls Daisy and don't bother with the formal name. In the language of flowers, daisies symbolize affection, innocence, and trust. If a secret was to be kept, a posy of daisies sent to the holder of the trust would ensure that the message was kept private.

The simple, harmonious structure and sweet face of the daisy make it one of the world's best-loved plants.

The simple, harmonious structure and sweet face of the daisy make it one of the world's best-loved plants and a lovely flower to press. Our personal favourites for pressing are the common *Bellis perennis* to be found on all but the best kept lawns. We also love the Mexican fleabane (*Erigeron karvinskianus*). This is the one that will grow through the cracks in the paving stones. The flowers start white and turn a rosy pink then lilac just before they die. It flowers joyfully and profusely all summer long, and it is fine to pull up some plants with roots and all to press because there will soon be too many, and what else will you do with them? We scattered some seeds about on the cobbles in the yard and up came the daisies. They can tolerate some shade and they neither want nor need rich soil. They are not troubled by disease or insects and continue to flower until the first frosts.

Cleone

WEDDINGS

When working on weddings we always want to make sure our couples get the most out of their flowers, whether it's how they can repurpose them on the day or rearranging them into recycled jars for their guests to take away at the end of the evening. Since we started pressing flowers, we have suggested pressing as an idea for preserving bouquets and table flowers to make everlasting artworks.

Many couples are approaching their weddings with a more sustainable mindset, so it's exciting for us to be able to discuss creative ideas on how to approach the floral elements to maximize the use of flowers. Using pressed flowers is also a lovely opportunity to incorporate floral details into the design of the wedding itself, from invitations to table settings and decor, and as a lasting keepsake.

INVITATIONS

Adding individual pressed flowers to your invitations is a pretty way to set your floral theme from day one. If you would like to do this, make a mock-up of one first with your flower of choice before you send the text invitations to print, to make sure you have allowed enough space on the layout to glue all the flowers into place later.

PLACE SETTINGS

A pressed flower on each place setting is a simple and cost-effective detail that will make a big difference. Choose flowers that complement your table flowers. You will need tiny flower heads, buds, or dainty stems—daisies, forget-me-nots, violas, phlox, astrantia, and wildflowers are all perfect for this. Play around with placement and glue the flowers first, making sure you leave plenty of space for calligraphy.

TABLE NAMES

If creating pressed-flower pieces for each of your guests is too big a task, you could incorporate pressed flowers into your table settings by making table names with them. Choose a good-quality mount board or textured handmade paper—we like Khadi Paper in 640gsm, A6 size. Look for a slim, discrete holder so it doesn't interfere with your table decor.

We always recommend enlisting a calligrapher for table and place names; Instagram is a great source for finding suppliers. Have the names or numbers written first before adding the pressed flowers, for consistency. Choose flowers that will complement your wedding flowers in colour and shape.

PRESSED BOUQUET

If you would like to preserve your wedding bouquet, the most important thing to remember is that flowers are best pressed fresh. Keep your bouquet in water during your wedding day to keep them looking perky; ask your florist or your venue to have a jar of water at the ready, and be prepared to press the flowers the day after your wedding or as soon as you can. You never know where your bouquet might end up on the day, so it's a good idea to have a back-up plan. Ask your florist to hold back a selection of flowers from your bouquet so you can press them separately.

When planning your wedding flowers, choose varieties that you know will press well. Even if some are not ideal for pressing, no matter what the season, you can always include elements that are. You don't only have to do this with your feature flowers; talk to your florists about the delicate details—dainty spires and lacy umbellifers, pretty foliage and feathery grasses add texture and interest to your bouquet, and they will all press beautifully.

PRESSED TABLE FLOWERS

There was barely a flower left after my wedding—they were either given to our guests to take home in jam jars, or they were pressed. I took a few buckets of flowers home after dismantling the arrangements from the staircase and marquee and pressed them all on the kitchen table two days later.

Our favourite way to display pressed wedding flowers is to make individual compositions with each of the flowers to be hung as a set. Mine are mounted on A3 cream mount board and framed in chic black aluminium frames—they look crisp and modern. Together they evoke a sense of that glorious summer day in mid-July; the colours, shapes, and textures that made everything sing.

Alternatively, you can experiment with mixed compositions to make one pressed flower piece that captures the look and feel of your wedding. When creating these, more often than not less is more. It's easy to overcrowd your chosen surface. As you experiment with layout, take photographs so you can look over lots of options to compare compositions. Although layering often works for dainty stems, it is important to keep some clear white space for balance.

Story

ORCHID

It is a sin to press a rare, wild orchid. This much we know; they are too vulnerable to be squandered in this way. If you don't know your orchid varieties well, just leave them be. Not all native orchids are endangered, of course, but due to their short flowering season and a habit of disappearing from one spot, only to reappear somewhere quite different, they have a reputation of being incredibly precious. The little fragile friends that we find on chalky grasslands and meadows across the UK belong to the vast and varied family Orchidaceae, with around 28,000 species worldwide and more than 169,000 horticultural hybrids. Fifty-eight of these grow wild in the UK.

Like most people I had two grandmothers, one of whom was the cosy type, a Yorkshire lass called Brenda Mayhew. She had six children and I was one of her fifteen grandchildren. During the war she kept her family going by growing vegetables, raising chickens and geese for eggs and, when they stopped laying, for the pot, she kept bees for honey and fattened a pig named Percy. Every year Percy was miraculously transformed back into a squealing piglet again, and pork and ham appeared at the table. Granny Mayhew was a gifted baker, a wonderful cook, and a marvellous gardener; she always found time for the flowers as well as the vegetables. Then there was the other granny—a very different kettle of fish. Audrey de Rougemont. She was a rather distant, exotic creature who lived in the Solomon Islands with her second husband. Unforgivably to my mother, she chose to visit the baby panda Chichi at London Zoo before coming to meet her first-born granddaughter. She wasn't very maternal, having had my father at eighteen. The first time I remember meeting her I was about three or four. She would have been in her early forties. She arrived from foreign parts, with her flaming hair, impossibly highly arched eyebrows, and painted scarlet lips, dressed in a chic two-piece suit. On her lapel she wore a silver brooch fashioned like a tiny vase, within which was an orchid flower. It was the most exotic thing I had ever seen—no relation to the English garden friends that I was used to. I have been fascinated by and slightly wary of orchids ever since.

Their name was given to them by the Greeks; rather surprisingly, the name *orkis* or *orchis* means testicle and refers to the pair of spherical tubers present in many European species. For this reason orchid tubers were collected and eaten across the Roman Empire in the vain hope of increasing sexual potency and fertility. Orchid names referring to this idea include priapiscus and satyrion.

By the Tudor era, the medical profession prescribed the consumption of orchid tubers for any and all complaints of a sexual nature. Perhaps this is the reason why some of our wild orchids have been driven to near extinction—although the reality is that it is more likely due to loss of habitat.

Prosthechea Cochleata
oncidium elegans
keighleyensis
oncidium (no name atm)
oncidium Hallii
pschopsis Mariposa
Brassia Verrucosa
Name (tbc)
Charlesworthii

In an unknown location somewhere on the Yorkshire Dales, the last surviving wild example of the lady's slipper orchid still grows. Believed to be extinct since 1917, a single plant was found by a botanist in 1930. It has the distinction of being the rarest wildflower in Britain. So highly valued is this precious flower, so prized and desired, that during its flowering season a guard pitches his tent near the orchid's habitat, with his sole purpose being to watch for possible thieves in the night. The lady's slipper, with its mustard-yellow pouch and deep red, winglike petals, is indeed a beauty. Seeds have been collected and taken to Kew where these notoriously difficult plants have been nurtured and propagated and then returned to the wild. In 2013, the lady's slipper orchid raised at Kew was exhibited at Chelsea Flower Show, with her bodyguard in attendance.

Orchids are the masters of disguise. No flower has more varieties that resemble critters, and the range of their mimicry is remarkable. There are orchids that resemble monkeys, butterflies, birds, bats, spiders, bees, lizards—really, any animal you can think of. They also use their scent as a device—scents that range from delicious to unbearably hideous. Orchids use every trick in the book to fool their pollinators. This is just as true of our native orchids in the UK as it is of their larger and more exotic cousins. Enchanting descriptions of the different kinds of orchids appear in *Gerard's Herbal Volume 1*, a 1,484-page illustrated *Herball*, or *Generall Historie of Plantes*, first published in 1597, such as, "White Birds Orchis: on the top whereof be white flowers resembling the shape or form of a small bird ready to fly, or a white butterfly with her wings spread abroad."

Orchids are the masters of disguise. No flower has more varieties that resemble critters.

As the British Empire expanded further abroad, exotic orchids were imported into the UK, where they were greeted with feverish enthusiasm. By the middle of the nineteenth century, the passion for orchids was so great that it got its own name: "Orchidelirium." The fact that they are difficult to grow and reproduce only increases their appeal to collectors and botanists.

There are plenty of orchid species that you can press. Slightly to our surprise, our first attempts with orchids were an unqualified success. I was in Sussex and went to visit my friend Rose Armstrong's astonishing orchid farm, housed in huge glasshouses under the curvaceous embrace of the South Downs. This remarkable place has, for the past 140 years, been the home of McBean's Orchid Farm.

It was late summer, the August Bank Holiday, to be exact, and the orchids were largely dormant. They lay green and mostly flowerless on great trays on wheels. Masses and masses of them. We walked around the glasshouses with Rose picking up flowers here and there and writing down the impossible Latin names for me.

I had brought a press with me and we laid the pickings between layers of blotting paper there and then in the glasshouses. Without much hope, I tightened the press and took it home. A few weeks later Amy and I opened the presses. The results were spectacular. The orchid's extraordinary, complex shapes had flattened out and become beautifully one-dimensional. They resembled exotic little creatures even more after pressing. We pranced around, delighted. Those first orchid pressings are still on the wall at the Jam-Jar studio, with my careful pencil-written notes of their outlandish names beside them. We had to wait a while to go back and do more. This time the steamy, heated glasshouses were full of colour, dripping with Spanish moss and giant ferns contrasting with the cold mist of a Sussex day in February. The massed orchids were magnificent to behold, lifting their exotic heads in the warm, moist air, shaking out their ruffles and curves like burlesque dancers in a painting by Toulouse-Lautrec—beautiful creatures from a far-off land, hunkered down under the South Downs, just outside Lewes.

TAKING CARE OF NATURE

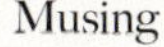

We wrote this book in the middle of the global Covid-19 pandemic that closed the world down in 2020. In the spring of that year there was an atmosphere of confusion, disbelief, and fear; some people thought it was a conspiracy, some locked themselves away from the world, terrified. Lonely and baffled, we all struggled with the end of a way of living that we had taken for granted. It took a curious kind of optimist to find a positive way of looking at this extraordinary world crisis.

But people are, on the whole, optimists; they want to find the good in things. As the usual rush hour to work slowed down to a trickle, we started to work, as much as we could, from home. We city dwellers found there was an extra hour or two in the day that we had normally spent underground fighting through the crowds to get to work. Instead we turned out in our thousands to our local parks, to nature reserves, and to the countryside, to watch a particularly warm and beautiful spring unfurl. For myself, I watched an oak tree turn from naked branches to full leaf over six weeks. I photographed it once a week from the same position, and while observing the annual miracle of rebirth I realized it was something I hadn't found the time to do since I was a child.

Many of us turned to nature to console us in our bereavement for the life we had known and carelessly believed was ours forever. As the sky emptied of planes, we became aware of marvellous birdsong that we had hardly noticed in other years against the roar of traffic in the city. But even as the urbanites walked out and watched with pleasure, with joy, the gift of spring, we put extra pressure on the few wild places that are left. I was thrilled to find these within a short walk from my London home where I have lived for thirty years, which I had never discovered before.

We all know that nature, flowers, and trees act as a solace and comfort to the troubled mind. Gardeners are famously some of the longest-living and happiest people on the planet, but nature is under serious threat today from over-population and from climate change. As we rediscover nature and fall in love, we run the risk of placing it in greater danger.

Isabella Tree, the author of the enormously successful book *Wilding*, tells the inspiring story of the transformation of her husband's family estate in Sussex, from intensive farming to a landscape wholly handed back to nature. As they allowed the land to recover on their estate, they introduced animals to try to recreate the Sussex countryside of a thousand years before, and were rewarded with a massive return in insects, birds, and butterflies that flocked to the land they left undisturbed.

A darker side of the story emerged in May. When lockdown was lifted, people rushed to get to the countryside, to see this blooming, marvellous "rewilding" miracle taking place. The Knepp Estate was swamped with visitors, who, when the car parks were full, parked on the grass verges and in neighbours' driveways, so hungry were they to catch a glimpse of the everyday miracle of spring. Visitor numbers increased tenfold. The same happened in areas of outstanding natural beauty like the Lake District, which received three times the usual amount of visitors at that time of year. As people rushed to reconnect with nature they actually caused damage to what they had come to see. By straying off pathways and unleashing their dogs, the visitors disturbed nesting birds and trampled on rare wildflowers and sapling trees. We cannot apportion blame too quickly here, but we do need to address the increased interest and need that people have for nature.

There is a move in the UK by a charity called buglife.org.uk to create something called B-line—nearly 400,000 acres of joined-up corridors of wildflowers to create a continuous

network for our pollinators to travel and traverse to every corner of the country. The three 1-metre- (1-yard-) wide paths of wildflower planting are enough for our invertebrates to survive in. We know that urban bees do very well, especially in London, because of all our green spaces and parks, and our little joined-up back gardens, which create a natural B-line for the busy worker bees who fly up to 3 miles a day collecting nectar and pollinating plants as they go. Even the neglected gardens overgrown with out-of-control buddleia and bindweed are just as useful to the pollinators as the more carefully planted ones.

Our British countryside has been depleted by overgrazing and intensive farming. A horrifying 97 per cent of wildflower habitat has been swept away by modern agriculture and building development since the 1940s, and with it we have put our pollinators at risk. But even as these grim figures emerge, there is a growing awareness of what needs to be done. It is not unusual now to find a corridor of wildflowers at the edges of fields of grain as farmers, who, after all, are most conscious of the seasons and the beauties of nature, try to save our wildlife while still making a living. Not always the easiest of combinations.

It makes me very sad to read how numbers of wildflowers have declined in my lifetime, but it is also very pleasing to see that we humans have finally understood the importance of protecting our precious wildlife, and how many people are working tirelessly to make sure they are around for many future generations to enjoy. Nature is always clever and will inevitably find places to continue her important business.

It is something of an irony that motorway verges, arguably one of the highest areas of carbon emissions, have become the surprising hosts of masses of wildflowers. Never mown or sprayed or interfered with, the grassy borders of a fast-flowing road are often buzzing with pollinators and bright with wildflowers, elder, and rambling roses.

Project

LIGHTBOX COMMISSION

Recently we were asked to make a lightbox with English garden flowers to be displayed in a private home. The commission was inspired by the pressed-flower windows we created for Sketch. Making a permanent pressed-flower piece to be lit with artificial light presented a new set of challenges as we knew this would accelerate the rate at which the flowers would fade.

We thought about which specimens retain their colour well and which faded in aesthetically pleasing ways. As an experiment for the Sketch windows, we had made a 40cm (16 inch) square sample piece using two layers of Perspex in between which pressed flowers were secured with tape. This sample has been propped up against the window of our studio with light flooding in from behind for just over three years. Except for the petals of the field poppy, which have held onto their colour, most of the flowers have faded considerably. But even as the colours have softened, it has enhanced the structure and tonality of each specimen, and evolved into an arguably more beautiful piece as a whole.

We also referred back to the pressed-flower wallpaper piece we made for *Rakesprogress* magazine (see page 96), which is framed behind plain glass with no UV protection. It has been exposed to daylight for even longer, so we can use it to monitor how different species change over time. We are often surprised when we suddenly notice a specimen has become completely bleached out, next to another which has barely changed at all. We are always learning from the process of flower pressing, especially by observing past experiments, which inform our decisions when selecting flowers for new works.

Showing these pieces to our clients did not discourage them from commissioning the artwork, they were intrigued by how their specimens would evolve over time. We agreed to refresh and replace the flowers at a later date if they faded too much, or were no longer to their liking, and we designed the lightbox structure accordingly. An ever-evolving piece. We had a lightbox made to our specifications with two sheets of Perspex to slide into the frame, one with a frosted finish, one clear.

Though we cannot entirely predict the rate at which the flowers will fade, we can choose flowers that we know usually keep their colour well, such as chocolate cosmos and astrantia, and others that even when faded have beautiful aesthetic qualities, such as sweet peas and butterfly ranunculus. We had been saving pressings specifically for this piece for several months. Along with deep purple astrantia and chocolate cosmos, we selected Shirley

poppies and hellebores for their depth of colour and strong shapes. Blue delphiniums added height, while pale, creamy coloured butterfly ranunculus and climbing sweet pea were added for their shape and movement, along with pale-lilac clematis and drifts of jasmine and honeysuckle.

We realized we had created a real *hortus siccus*—a dried garden. By subjecting the flowers to the light source, we have made the very nature of their fragility and fading part of the piece. Perhaps this is the ultimate celebration of the ephemeral nature of the pressed flower.

I had the pleasure of delivering and installing this piece myself. It was great fun to see the delighted reaction of our clients as the lights were switched on. They said it was like looking through a window onto a garden, which was exactly what we had set out to achieve. It will be interesting to observe how this piece changes over time.

Story

NATURE PRINTING

Scrolling, as you do, through Instagram one day, we happened across the marvellous work of Rachel Dein. Fascinated, Amy and I made the journey across town to Rachel's studio in her home in North London to meet her and discuss the possibility of her making some pieces for us to sell through the JamJar Edit, our online shop. We found her in the garden, looking for species to press on a fine spring morning. In her house, she was embarking on much bigger pieces and there were examples of her work everywhere. Whether it was a wavering line of grasses, a single snowdrop, or enormous branches of plane leaves with pendulous seedheads, everything was such a pleasure to look at. We particularly loved the casts of herbs and vegetables such as artichokes, carrots, and beetroot from Roland Blanc's gardens at Le Manoir aux Quat'Saisons.

Rachel's work has evolved from the early nature printers; she makes casts of plants and flowers in plaster and clay. She records the structure and shape of the plant in miraculous detail. In many ways, her work reflected our own adventures with pressing flowers; we found we had masses to discuss. The great difference between our work and Rachel's is that, once she has pressed the flowers into the clay and made her impression, the flower is completely lost, but it has left a permanent record. Like pressed flowers, the plant that would, in the natural way of things, be dead shortly after it has flowered, lives on, perfectly preserved, but in another form. We loved the fact that most of Rachel's work is monochrome, rendered in creamy plaster so the flower impressions are like beautiful, ethereal ghosts.

Rendered in creamy plaster, the flower impressions are like beautiful little ethereal ghosts.

This technique is all about printing directly from nature. During the Middle Ages, nature prints were made by botanists and herbalists who wanted to record a plant and note its various properties. In its most simple form, a plant would be covered in ink then pressed down onto paper to produce an accurate, if rather crude, reproduction.

One of the earliest examples of nature printing was found in Dioscorides' *De Materia Medica*, an encyclopedia of plants and their medicinal properties. This text was widely used for 1,500 years after Dioscorides' death. The Islamic manuscript, dated 1228, had been copied in Anatolia or northern Syria by a scholar named Behnam the Christian. It contained an insert with the first known nature print of leaves and taproots. It is possible that this beautiful specimen was not contemporary to the manuscript, but it is, without doubt, very old and is generally accepted to be the first example of nature printing.

Leonardo da Vinci also made one known nature print of a sage leaf, with text explaining his method in mirror writing. It appears in Folio 197, verso *Il Codice Atlantico* (1478) and is singularly beautiful.

In 1737, in the USA, Benjamin Franklin cleverly used casts of real leaves printed on a copper press for bank notes. The unique structure of the nature-printed leaves meant that it was very difficult to copy the notes and produce counterfeit paper money.

But it was not until the nineteenth century that nature printing really got sophisticated. The person credited with perfecting the process was Alois Auer, a highly educated Austrian printer, inventor, and botanical illustrator. He was director of the Imperial Printing House in Vienna and his first experiments with this new form of printing were to reproduce lace, but he quickly moved on to plants. Using soft lead, he created accurate impressions of the plants from which he could make prints. Auer called his new process *Naturselbstdruck* and described it thus:

> An invention for creating by means of its original self—in a swift and simple manner-plates for printing copies of plants, materials, lace… containing the most delicate profundities or elevations… in various colours with one single impression… by the ordinary letter press (or) copper plate press… without the aid of drawing or engraving.

The printing process had several stages, first the plant was pressed between softened lead and a sheet of steel, leaving an impression in the lead. Once an impression had been captured, Auer could make the electroplated copperplate, from which multiple prints could be made.

Auer was rightly proud of his achievements, so it was extremely galling when William Bradbury and Frederick Evans made some tiny adaptations to his methods and patented the process as their own. Particularly as Bradbury's son, Henry, had spent months of what we would now call an internship with Auer, learning his methods and observing his work. In 1855 both Henry Bradbury and Alois Auer printed books on nature printing. By including coloured inks to his *The Ferns of Great Britain*, Bradbury's work was more vibrant than Auer's *Hysiotypia Plantarum Austriacarum Der Naturselbstdruck…der Pflanzen* (*Physiotypes of Austrian Plants, Nature pressed*). But both were masterpieces in their own way, showing faithful and accurate reproductions of plants in a way never seen before, except in single-pressed specimens.

Perhaps Bradbury did feel guilty about plagiarizing his master's work; in any case he committed suicide by drinking prussic acid in 1860, and with Auer's death in 1869, followed by the arrival of photography soon afterwards, nature printing as a commercial practice ceased to exist—although many artists are inspired by their work and continue to practise nature printing, as an art form, to this day.

For ourselves, as we continued our adventures with pressing flowers, we began to worry about the inevitable leaching of colour in the pressed-flower pieces we were making. We wanted the people who bought our artworks to enjoy and even celebrate the changes over time as the pressed flowers slowly faded in colour, but there will always be some clients who want everything to remain the same. Refreshing a piece with new pressings is one solution, but one year, at Frieze Masters, an annual London Art Fair showcasing the best art galleries and significant masterpieces from around the world, we thought we might have found another. A longstanding fan of our work,

antiquarian Rupert Wace introduced us to the maverick genius who is Adam Lowe. Adam is the director and founder of Factum Foundation and its sister company Factum Arte, based in Madrid. The Factum Foundation "was established to demonstrate the importance of documenting, monitoring, studying, recreating and disseminating the world's cultural heritage through the rigorous development of high-resolution recording and dematerialisation techniques."

Tentatively, we approached Adam about whether he might consider looking at using his groundbreaking techniques to create a facsimile of a pressed flower in 3D—something that very closely resembled the actual piece, but would not change or lose colour over time. Adam responded with characteristic enthusiasm. It turned out that he was a massive fan of nature printing and the idea of reproducing our pressed specimens excited him as much as it did us. Rupert, Amy, and I spent a couple of days at the foundation where Adam shared with us books on nature printing from his enormous library. We were overwhelmed by the sheer volume of the work being undertaken in the enormous, rambling factory and the variety of disciplines being employed by his incredible team. Here we saw exact replicas of the Seti tomb, Boucher's portrait of Madame de Pompadour, and a 3D scan of a 900-year-old oak from Windsor Great Park miniaturized as a perfect replica in bronze. A Van Gogh *Sunflowers* lost in World War II, was being reproduced with actual Van Gogh brushstrokes from other paintings of the sunflowers; Amy even

got popped into a mad spacey-looking machine to be 3D-scanned herself! The process was fascinating; naked, white, embossed prints came first and then, through a buildup in layers of ink, the delicate texture of the petals appeared. Colour was added last, with a colour-checking scan to make sure the reproductions accurately matched the originals.

On our return to London, we set about creating an archive of pressed flowers for Factum Arte to scan. We wanted to send our most precious specimens. When we went to pack up the flowers, we found we had inadvertently pressed a few tiny caterpillar eggs that had hatched out and snacked on the flowers in our archive boxes, reducing some of the best Shirley poppies to lace. While they were rather beautiful in themselves, the whole archive had to be carefully gone over for any lurking bug life before being dispatched.

A few weeks later a package arrived from Factum. The 3D images went above and beyond our wildest expectations. Holding the sample prints in our hands was a thrilling moment.

As we continue our conversations with Adam, we are extremely excited about all the possibilities of 3D plant replicas. Normally we only have one of each precious pressing, but having scans means we can reuse our favourite specimens and super-scale plants. We sense all sorts of new adventures with this most modern form of nature printing. We will never stop making artworks out of real pressed flowers, but here is another exciting string to our bow that has limitless possibilities.

Story

TRANSIENCE

Working with pressed flowers has allowed us to explore the idea of creating permanence from the fleeting cycles of nature. We have the chance to halt the process of deterioration and preserve flowers indefinitely. But quite early in our flower-pressing journey we realized we were going to have to address the fact that the vibrant colours we had preserved would, inevitably, fade over time. The work was going to change, colour would be lost, but form and structure would remain, bringing with it a new sort of beauty. This is an accepted part of our work, which should be celebrated rather than regretted.

We felt slightly reassured by the fact that artists like Damien Hirst, whose art—particularly the "Nature History" series in which he preserved creatures in formaldehyde and exhibited them in glass cases—was also subject to the vagaries of natural change. His work deals with the transience of life and the fragility of existence in real species; his methods do not stop deterioration, they simply slow the process, but nevertheless the preserved creatures will, and do, deteriorate over time. Many of his works have to be refreshed or replaced. However, his does not take away from the validity of each piece.

Nothing lasts forever.

The Japanese have a tradition of celebrating nature called "Hanami," which literally means "looking at flowers." It is a tradition in which people take the time to enjoy the brief flowering of blossom and contemplate the evanescence of nature. For centuries they waited for the winter to end and longed for the arrival of the plum *ume* blossom, heralding, as it should, a good harvest and the summer ahead. Today Hanami is a national celebration of the more exotic cultivars and showy cherry blossom—*sakura*. People picnic under the trees drinking liberal amounts of saki, celebrating the arrival of spring.

Even as the Japanese marvel at the cherry blossom, taking the time to "stand and stare," they are also contemplating the brevity of this spectacular moment. We, too, feel a stab of piercing grief or melancholy as we enjoy the fruit trees flowering in England. We know that in only a few days, almost as quickly as it came, the blossom will be over. This year it was a brisk cold breeze that took out the pear blossom in my garden, suddenly the sky was filled with a flurry of snowy petals that fell and covered the ground. Seeing this, we are reminded that beauty is evanescent; and we are also reminded of our own mortality.

As florists, we are all too aware of the ephemeral beauty of flowers. We make gorgeous and extravagant pieces that last for one day and are then taken down and lost forever. One bitingly cold New Year's Day we went, rather grumpy and hungover, to take down a gorgeous wedding in Mayfair. The last guests had apparently left only moments before we arrived. Amid the detritus, the empty glasses, half-eaten pieces of cake, and discarded napkins, the flowers still looked perfect. We dismantled everything, loaded up the flowers and drove out to the city dump, where, with freezing hands thrust deep into our pockets, we watched the thousands of flowers and foliage being scooped up by a mechanical digger. We felt depressed and wondered why we did our job at all; the whole thing suddenly felt wasteful and pointless. A few days later the photographs arrived, and with them the realization that what we do is significant precisely because the beauty of flowers is so fleeting. The moment had been captured. We had helped to make a precious memory, which will, in time, also fade. The time and trouble we spent should not be considered worthless or wasteful, but precious and important.

Today when an event or wedding is over we eschew the city dump and rush the flowers back to Peacock Yard. It's a bit like the emergency room as we dive into the compost bags to rescue flowers, anything that is still alive and suitable is pressed. The dying flowers are then transmuted into their second existence.

Story

A CONVERSATION WITH NICK KNIGHT

"[A pressed flower's] permanence goes against most cultural visions of flowers, which is this very transient beauty."

Nick Knight is a contemporary artist who has been similarly captivated by the fleeting beauty of flowers in his work. Nick became fascinated with the aesthetic qualities of the pressed plant after being introduced to the herbarium at the Natural History Museum, while he was working on an exhibition exploring mankind's relationship with plants in the early 1990s. I had a wonderful conversation with him about the time he spent in the herbarium.

Flowers are often represented in a transient, poetic way throughout art history. The Dutch still-life paintings of the seventeenth century, for example, often depict wilting flowers to symbolize life and death, or the ephemeral. What surprised Nick about the pressings, and inspired him to take a break from fashion photography to focus on this project, was that, up until now, he had only experienced art's preoccupation with this moment of a flower's brief life and imminent death. But in the pages of the herbarium he found quite the opposite—permanent statements of beauty. *"I liked that confidence it gave them. They had the permanence of modernism about them. I think that set them apart for me."*

Nick spent three-and-a-half years examining the six million specimens, looking for the most beautiful ones to photograph. This was to become his stunning book of just forty-five photographs, *Flora*. Although the specimens had been collected, pressed, mounted, and archived by botanists, Nick was moved by the way the scientific approach to delivering the required information had manifested itself in a very artistic way. *"If ever you wanted to find reason for believing in a higher force, you'd probably find it in an herbarium because some of (the specimens) are so incredibly funny, and beautiful, and charming, and full of wit—which you don't expect when you (look at) flower pressings. They don't look anything like the flowers and plants you know."*

The thing that fascinated me in this conversation was how he was able to express the modern aesthetic qualities of these centuries-old specimens. It resonated with the way we approach flower pressing at JamJar. We have always aspired to elevate this scientific practice into a relevant and modern art form. *"What attracted me the most was the fact that these plants primarily did not look like plants. They made me think of completely different things: some were like feathers—but feathers of neon, laser-drawn, exquisitely refined and breathtakingly delicate. Others were like urban plants, architecturally precise, like cities viewed from the air, infinitely complex. Many were joyful splashes of colour like childrens' paintings, carefree happy nonsense."* – Nick Knight, *Flora*

—

I was raised in a beautiful house in Sussex, called Long House. My father was a wonderful gardener; flowers crowded out of beds and onto paths. Clematis, honeysuckle, and roses climbed up and tumbled over soft, rosy brick walls. Beyond the walls were deep woods, filled with dappled light and wild garlic. As children we would pick wildflowers to put in jam jars on the kitchen table. They grew at different times of the year—primroses in early spring, bluebells in May, and spotty scarlet mushrooms in the autumn. I can hear and smell it now, the rich mixture of beeswax and woodsmoke, honeysuckle and moss, the crackle of fires, the drip, drip, drip from the leaky roof into tin buckets, the lazy buzzing of a captive bee against the diamond panes of glass.

Naturally I could not wait to get away from this bucolic idyll as a teenager. I fell in love with the city, with its secret places and histories tucked beside shimmering modernity. The people, the society, the possibilities, the parties, and the sheer speed of life were irresistible to me. Even so, for many years, Long House remained a retreat where I escaped city life and could reconnect with nature.

I started Take 2 Model Management in 1982, which became one of the leading modelling agencies in London, and traded successfully until 2009; I found the fashion industry was changing fast in a way I no longer admired. I craved a simpler life, arranging flowers for people who like what I like: beautiful and seasonal flowers. After thirty years of running the agency, I started JamJar at the kitchen table in 2009. I wanted to keep it simple—a few contract flowers and local deliveries in jam jars. Never could I have imagined the journey it would take me on or the wonderful people I would meet along the way.

Amy and I met in 2014 when she arrived at our studio in a Dickensian yard in Kennington. The day Amy came to work with us was a turning point for the little business we call JamJar Flowers.

Amy Fielding

I grew up in Warrington, a large town in the northwest of England. My dad's stories of living life as a Mod in the sixties sparked my fascination with the era and my love of modernist design. I like clean lines, simple forms, and clean white space. Modernism, for me, has somewhat manifested in the pages of this book. Through the process of pressing, I see flowers transformed into compositions of minimalist lines and shapes; blocks of colour and texture. Floristry became very exciting for me the moment we started pressing flowers.

Working for renowned fashion photographer Nick Knight made a lasting impression on me when I first moved to London, and ultimately inspired me to work with flowers. There were always flowers in the studio—beautiful, elegant, unfussy. I would buy hydrangeas or roses from the flower cart outside Stella McCartney's Bond Street shop in the summer and arrange them carefully in clear glass vases. Nick would arrive with buckets full of the most deliciously scented and beautiful roses I had ever seen; hand-picked from his garden to be photographed. They were treated with as much care as any of the models he worked with.

I later worked as a producer, and fashion, for me, became increasingly unfulfilling. I wanted to create things with my own hands. After reading about JamJar in a fashion magazine, I rode my scooter across London one sunny June afternoon to the studio. It was a breath of fresh air, buzzing with activity. Buckets of flowers everywhere, kettle boiling, radio blaring, and Melissa's booming voice telling tales. Bursting with colour and scent, the studio was absolute chaos—in the best possible way. I knew I could introduce some much-needed calm and order. I felt could be useful.

Never would I have imagined that our brief chat that day would lead to such a wonderful creative partnership. Melissa and I launched JamJar Edit together in 2017, our online shop—a marriage of our two distinct styles. It was Melissa who lured me in and set me on this floral adventure, for which I am forever grateful. I am still in awe of her boundless energy, creative vision, and extraordinary ability to always look forwards.

PICTURE CREDITS

All photographs © JamJar Flowers except: pp.5, 8, 10, 12 © Helen Cathcart; pp. 14–17 © Mulberry; pp.19, 20, 21, 22–23, 24, 26, 28, 29, 31 © Helen Cathcart; p.33 © G. Dagli Orti/© NPL – DeA Picture Library/ Bridgeman Images; pp34–39, 43, 44 © Helen Cathcart; pp.46–47 © Yolanda Chiaramello; pp.48, 50, 52–53, 54–57, 59, 60, 62–63, 64, 67, 69, 70, 72–83, 85, 86 © Helen Cathcart; p.96 © Jane Hilton; pp.98–99, 100 © Gabriel Carasso; pp.102–3, 105, 106, 109, 113 © Helen Cathcart; pp.114, 115, 116, 117, 118 © Yolanda Chiaramello; p.119 © Jen Harrison Bunning; pp.121, 123, 124, 127, 128–129, 130, 132, 135, 136–143, 145 © Helen Cathcart; p.147 © Bridgeman Art Library/National Galleries of Scotland; pp.148, 151, 153, 154, 157, 159, 166, 168, 171, 172–173 © Helen Cathcart; p.175 © The Trustees of the Natural History Museum, London; pp.179, 180 © Helen Cathcart; p.183 © AKG Images; p.184 © Helen Cathcart; p.186 © Francesca Morgan; pp.187, 188, 189, 191 © Helen Cathcart; pp.195, 196–197 © Helen Cathcart; p.199 © The Natural History Museum/Alamy Stock Photo; p.201 © The Trustees of the British Museum; p.203 © British Library Board. All Rights Reserved/Bridgeman Images; p.205 © President and Fellows of Harvard College, Houghton Library, MS Am 1118.11; p.207 © Courtesy of the California Academy of Sciences; p.209 © Courtesy of the Armitt Trust; p.211 © Archives of the Princely Palace–To learn more about Princess Grace's living legacy, visit Princess Grace Foundation-USA, www.pgfusa.org; pp.212–213 © Kasia Wozniak; pp.214–216 © Helen Cathcart; p.217 © Kasia Wozniak; pp.218, 219, 220, 222, 223, 224, 226 © Helen Cathcart; p.229 © Kasia Wozniak; p.233 © Laurence Mackman / Alamy Stock Photo; pp.234, 235 ©Kasia Wozniak; pp.237, 238, 240, 241, 242, 243, 244, 247, 248–253, 255 © Helen Cathcart; p.256 © Florilegius/Bridgeman Images; pp.258–261, 262, 263, 264 © Helen Cathcart; p.266 Rachel Dein, Spring: lilac, dicentra, symphytum, Welsh poppy, iberis, epimidium and hellebore © Andrew Montgomery; p270 Elevated Printing Samples © Factum Arte, 2018; p.269 Rachel Dein process © Andrew Montgomery; p.273 © Shutterstock/lydiarei; p.275 Nick Knight © Nick Knight, Nympheaceae, Flora Series, 1994–1997; pp.276, 278, 280, 287 © Helen Cathcart

TEXT COPYRIGHTS

p.88 "By the Seaside," Sir John Betjeman; p.218 "Tulips," from "Ariel," by Sylvia Plath, Faber & Faber Ltd

—

It has been a fascinating journey of discovery to research, write, and illustrate the stories and projects that make up the pages of this book. It is impossible to overestimate the contribution our co-conspirator India Cooper has made to this process. Her meticulous and tactful editing skills have helped immensely to shape these pages. India read all our offerings and advised us on everything from botanical knowledge, to structure, grammar, and punctuation. We are immensely grateful for her painstaking and thoughtful input, her patience and intelligence, all of which inspired us to keep on going.

Thank you to everyone else who helped us bring this book to press. First, most grateful thanks to both of our partners, Charlie Alexander and Tim Fielding, for their endless enthusiasm for the project. To our fellow Jammers, Talena Rolfe and Ella Bandtock, who encouraged us to write the proposal when everything went quiet in the spring of 2020, and who listened to our endless fussing. To Melissa's reader, Joe Alexander, for his edit suggestions on grammar, sense, and content. To Daisy Garnett for letting us use her lovely garden, for the delicious mulberry ice cream and gardening advice. To the Hibbert family at Thyme for letting us have a gorgeous cottage to work in. To Helen Cathcart for her wonderful photography, Hazel Eriksson and Helena Caldon, our kind and patient editors, Zoë Bather for the book design, and Sarah Hopper for sourcing wonderful images to illustrate our botanical histories and heroines; thank you for understanding and translating our vision. Special thanks to our agent Julian Alexander, of The Soho Agency, and of course Myles Archibald at William Collins for believing a book about pressed flowers could come to something.

To you all, thank you… It's been an amazing adventure,
and actually a dream come true.

READER'S DIGEST ENCYCLOPAEDIA OF GARDEN PLANTS AND FLOWERS
Geoffrey Smith's World of Flowers
Pressed Plant
PANTONE
100 Postcards

labels
Stationary